Christmas

The Annual of Christmas Literature and Art

Christmas

Christmas

The Annual of Christmas Literature and Art

FOUNDED BY RANDOLPH E. HAUGAN, EDITOR VOLUMES ONE THROUGH FIFTY

Volume Fifty-four

Augsburg Publishing House
Minneapolis, Minnesota

Christmas Gospel 5

Christmas Music 30

Christmas Customs 39

Christmas Classic 46

Christmas Nostalgia 54

Table of Contents

Editorial Staff: Leonard Flachman, Karen Walhof, Jennifer Fast.

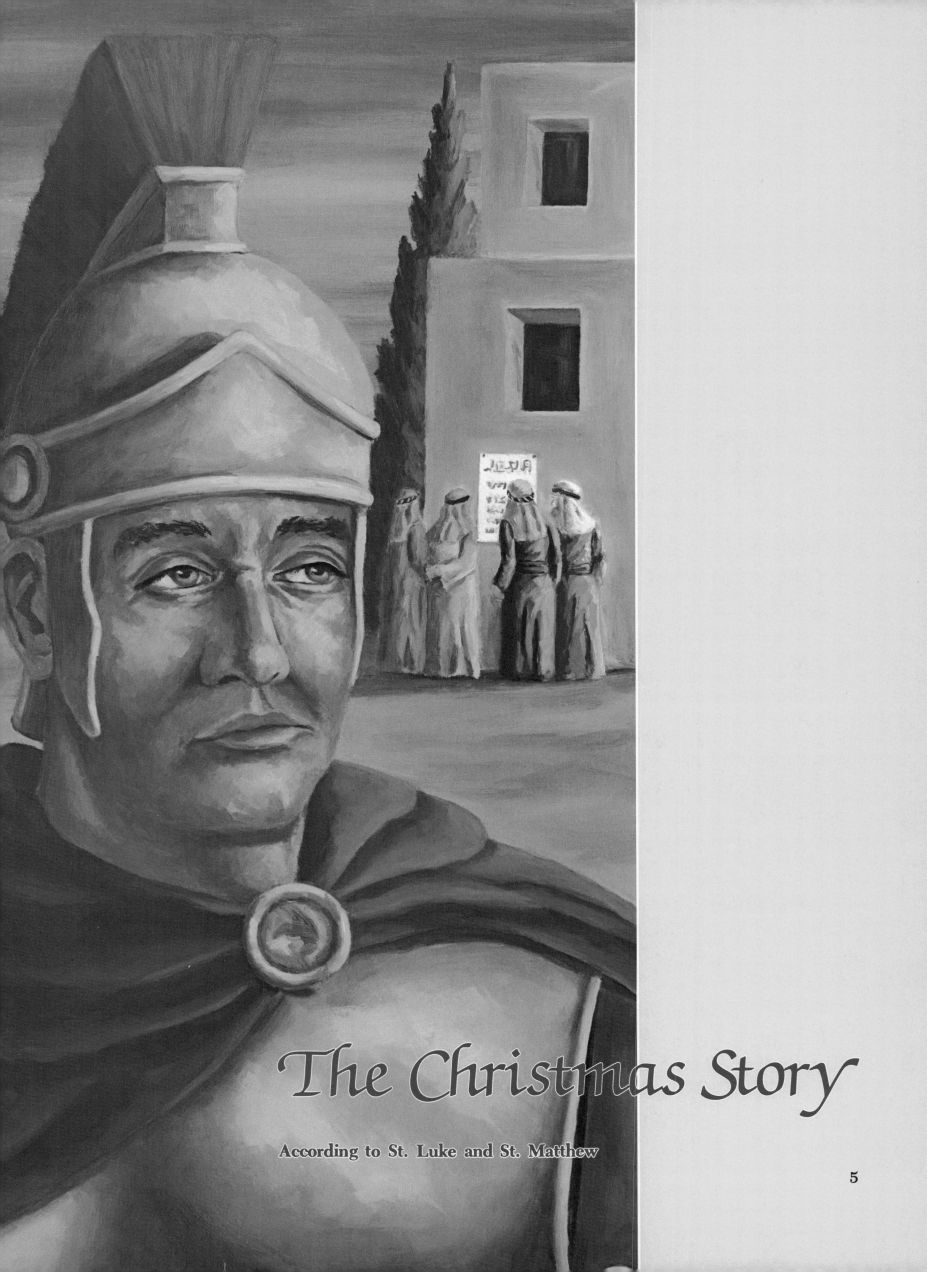

The Christmas Story

According to St. Luke and St. Matthew

And it came to pass in those days that a decree went out from Caesar Augustus that all the world should be registered.

This census first took place while Quirinius was governing Syria.

And all went to be registered, everyone to his own city.

And Joseph also went up from Galilee, out of the city of Nazareth, into Judea, to the city of David, which is called Bethlehem, because he was of the house and lineage of David, to be registered with Mary, his betrothed wife, who was with child.

And so it was, that while they were there, the days were completed that she should be delivered.

And she brought forth her firstborn son, and wrapped him in swaddling cloths, and laid him in a manger, because there was no room for them in the inn.

And there were in the same country shepherds living out in the fields, keeping watch over their flock by night.

And behold, an angel of the Lord stood before them, and the glory of the Lord shone around them, and they were greatly afraid.

And the angel said to them, "Do not be afraid, for behold, I bring you good tidings of great joy which will be to all people.

"For there is born to you this day in the city of David a Savior, who is Christ the Lord.

"And this will be the sign to you: You will find a babe wrapped in swaddling cloths, lying in a manger."

And suddenly there was with the angel a multitude of the heavenly host praising God and saying: "Glory to God in the highest, and on earth peace, good will toward men!"

And so it was, when the angels had gone away from them into heaven, that the shepherds said to one another, "Let us now go to Bethlehem and see this thing that has come to pass, which the Lord has made known to us."

And they came with haste and found Mary and Joseph, and the babe lying in a manger.

And when they had seen it, they made widely known the saying which was told them concerning this child.

And all those who heard it marveled at those things which were told them by the shepherds.

But Mary kept all these things and pondered them in her heart.

And the shepherds returned, glorifying and praising God for all the things that they had heard and seen, as it was told to them.

ow after Jesus was born in Bethlehem of Judea in the days of Herod the king, behold, Wise Men from the East came to Jerusalem, saying, "Where is he who has been born King of the Jews? For we have seen his star in the East and have come to worship him."

When Herod the king had heard these things, he was troubled, and all Jerusalem with him.

And when he had gathered all the chief priests and scribes of the people together, he inquired of them where the Christ was to be born.

And they said to him, "In Bethlehem of Judea, for thus it is written by the prophet:

'And you, Bethlehem, in the land of Judah,
Are not the least among the rulers of Judah;
For out of you will come a Ruler
Who will shepherd my people Israel.'"

Then Herod, when he had secretly called the Wise Men, determined from them what time the star appeared.

And he sent them to Bethlehem and said, "Go and search diligently for the young child, and when you have found him, bring back word to me, that I may come and worship him also."

When they had heard the king, they departed; and behold, the star which they had seen in the East went before them, till it came and stood over where the young child was.

When they saw the star, they rejoiced with exceeding great joy.

And when they had come into the house, they saw the young child with Mary his mother, and fell down and worshiped him. And when they had opened their treasures, they presented gifts to him: gold, frankincense and myrrh.

And being warned by God in a dream that they should not return to Herod, they departed for their own country another way.

10

nd when they had departed, behold, an angel of the Lord appeared to Joseph in a dream, saying, "Arise, take the young child and his mother, flee to Egypt, and stay there until I bring you word; for Herod will seek the young child to destroy him."

When he arose, he took the young child and his mother by night and departed into Egypt, and was there until the death of Herod, that it might be fulfilled which was spoken by the Lord through the prophet, saying, "Out of Egypt I have called my son."

But when Herod was dead, behold, an angel of the Lord appeared in a dream to Joseph in Egypt, saying, "Arise, take the young child and his mother, and go into the land of Israel, for those who sought the young child's life are dead."

And he arose, took the young child and his mother, and came into the land of Israel.

12

Christmas in the Nation's Capital

SCOTT LUCAS

J ust arriving in Washington is captivating. Whether flying out of a low-lying cloud or motoring over a rise on one of the many arterial land paths, you are met by the immediately recognized and welcome sight of the Washington Monument and, perhaps, the glistening white dome of the nation's Capitol jutting from the surrounding rooftops and trees. A lump forms in your throat as well as a slight constriction in your breast as you realize you are about to tread upon history—Christmas in the nation's capital.

Customs dating back to prerevolutionary days and more recently established annual events combine to give the city its unique Christmas character. Some public and private homes will be carefully and traditionally decked out early in the season; others will be decorated on the same dates that have been observed for generations. Always, you are aware of those who have come before and those who are certain to follow. The feelings of tradition and history are inescapable.

The Washington metropolitan area is split almost diagonally by the Potomac River basin and is ringed by the Capital Beltway. Three million people call the area home. The District of Columbia, centered in this sprawling megapolis of small interwoven communities, claims almost 700,000 of these people as citizens. And yet as you travel about the city and its environs, you'll feel the pride of individuality, whether it be in suburban Bethesda or mid-city Dupont Circle, Fairfax, Virginia, or New Carrollton, Maryland. All are drawn to the core of the city proper by the emotional, spiritual, and common celebration of Christmas. From the wide and spacious Pennsylvania Avenue to the quaint cobblestone streets of Georgetown, from the casual yet jubilant influence of Adams-Morgan to the quiet and lavishly decorated neighborhood of Spring Valley, and from the graceful elegance of the White House to the more sedate, church-oriented celebrations, you can feel Christmas in the air.

The first week in December brings only hints of the Christmas season

and its accompanying spirit. The days grow shorter, of course, and the sky dissolves into a melange of dull colors. Rain is more frequent than snow this time of year, but weather aberrations become the norm. An eight-inch blanket of snow may be quickly followed by a week of springlike days with temperatures in the high sixties. But, whatever the weather, Christmas approaches!

The traditional Pageant of Peace opens each December to welcome citizens from near and far to glory in the festival of lights and colors on the Ellipse behind the White House. More than 5000 people turn out the first week in December in late morning to see the giant National Christmas Tree topped. The topping is traditionally performed by the vice-president's wife. Held aloft in a National Park Service cherry picker, she places the crowning ornament on the 35-foot-tall tree. Fifty-seven smaller trees, one for each American state and territory, are decorated and lighted this same week. The giant national tree is lit before many thousands of onlookers in an evening ceremony by the president of the United States. Twelve thousand watts of specially designed lighting explode with brilliance at his touch. The early evening spectacle, just prior to Christmas week, is viewed by millions worldwide. In the weeks that follow native Washingtonians are vastly outnumbered as tens of thousands of visitors flock to witness this Christmas spectacle. One can see the grizzled countenances of legislators soften as they escort their young constituents past the manger scene or grazing reindeer; the power politics and blustering winds of demand seem to be checked like coats at the arched entrance. During the month, the sounds of live staged performances, dancing, and accompanying music permeate the crisp evening air for blocks. It's almost impossible to find a frown here.

The White House calendar is jammed with events, some traditional and some not so traditional. Understandably, to host the president

Photos: (opposite) The Capitol. (right) National Christmas Tree and Washington Monument, Pageant of Peace, horse and buggy on the Ellipse.

and first lady is a security nightmare. Therefore, many, if not all, of their public activities are televised live or taped for later viewing. You cannot be in Washington long and stay unaware of their presence at Christmastime. The occupants of the White House change from time to time, but the office of the presidency seems tailor-made for the celebration of and participation in Washington's Christmas season. From the White House the president and first lady involve themselves in the nation's Christmas festivities, by use of television and through the thousands of visitors who tour the home of the presidents. In December, the White House is trimmed and decorated like any other home, more fancily perhaps, but nevertheless reflecting those Christmas ideals and beliefs shared by the vast majority of Americans. The White House festivities run the gamut from social causes to splendid entertainment. White House concerts are held and televised. Also, the nationally televised Christmas celebration with the president in the old Pension Building has the possibility of becoming a new national tradition. Dozens of children, celebrity singers, local groups such as the Shiloh Baptist Church, and the U.S. Naval Academy Glee Club have participated in this celebration in the past.

Parties at the White House reflect the general compatibility of Christmas with almost any setting, but the favorite event seems to be the annual White House Christmas Party, where 400 children from 89 countries wedge into the East Room. They surround the White House Christmas tree, a stately pine decorated with an endless variety of ornaments, cookies even, and topped by the presidential seal. For this party, imagine the red-coated Marine Band playing "Frosty the Snowman," clowns, a prancing seven-foot candy cane, a Santa, and all those children's sparkling eyes. Imagine eight Christmas trees gracing the State Rooms with hundreds of poinsettia plants competing for attention. And think of all those children edging up to the State Dining Room tables for their share of chocolate

cookies and fruitcakes as entertainment echoes throughout the home. This party is certain to be a Christmas memory passed along by those who attend.

The mystical feeling you enjoy here at Christmas is not confined to the secular or the whimsical. Religious work is important as well. People of all races work together in an untold number of worthy projects, and people from every spot on earth who now reside in Washington respond to the needs of all people. Behind the day-to-day giving and caring you're more likely to find a church or religious organization than a government agency. Although the season of giving is not seasonal, in December, more than any other time of the year, the churches reach out in celebration, assistance, and ministry.

The metropolitan churches reach out to share their Christmas joy with the communty also. Those celebrations may take on the character of a family gathering, where small children participate in recitation and song. Or, those celebrations may be more formal, such as the African Methodist Episcopal Cathedral Choir's spirited presentation of the *Messiah.*

Major Pierre L'Enfant, when planning this capital city for the new republic with President George Washington, included in his proposals the request for a "great church for national purposes." Toward the close of the 19th century, a 57-acre parcel of land was secured on Mount St. Alban, the highest of hills near the Potomac River and within sight of the Capitol. Architects toiled diligently, and plans were delivered in 1907. That fall, the foundation stone, a stone brought from a field near Bethlehem, was placed into a larger one of American granite and tamped to ground with a gavel used by George Washington. Since that time, work has faltered but never failed, and "a house of prayer for all people" nears completion. The National Cathedral rises spectacularly, and at Christmas the majesty and ethereal beauty bespeaks magnificence. Awestruck, people stream in to participate in the Christmas activities, which cut across denominational lines and breathe new love and life into the hallowed stone. A stained glass lecture and tours go hand in hand with choral exhibitions. The annual Cathedral Choral Society concert presents the Cathedral Choir of Boys and Men and the National Symphony Brass Quintet; it simply should not be missed.

It is humanly impossible to see all of the things Washington has to offer at Christmas. For example, the Smithsonian Institution is a national treasury, "the country's attic," some wags venture, but certainly the grandest collection of galleries and museums known on earth. Building after building, acre after acre of display, offer history you can see and touch. So many facets of the American promise and dream are here that many scholars and craftspeople never finish in their lifetime the works they have begun to restore and assemble. They pass these chores gratefully and willingly to their protégés for the continuation of their work and hope. The collections really never will be finished. The Smithsonian Institution heralds America.

The holiday spirit pervades the Smithsonian, from the Air and Space Museum's lecture on "The Stars of Christmas" to the Hirshhorn Museum's "Holiday: A Celebration for Children," from the National Museum of American History's exhibit entitled "The Trees of Christmas" to the Renwick Gallery's series celebrating Christmas sweets, "Visions of Sugar Plums." The National Museum of American Art schedules holiday storytelling, puppet shows, and avant-garde films. Concerts, lunchtime lectures, free film theaters, gingerbread house construction demonstrations, holiday music performances by children's groups featuring worldwide favorites, and more are found here amongst the various indoor displays. Dancers, actors, mimes, musicians, and other artists are everywhere. Like Pied Pipers they seem irresistible and draw crowds to frolic behind them.

For a better idea of the scope, the unparalleled, almost unbelievable vastness of the collections found at the Smithsonian Institution, place yourself on the top steps of the Capitol and look West down the Mall toward the Washington Monument and the Lincoln Memorial. On your left in order will be the Air and Space Museum, the Hirshhorn Museum, the Arts and Industries Building, and the Smithsonian "Castle." On your right in order will be the masterful triangular newer East Building in front of the National Gallery of Art's older West Building, the Museum of Natural History, and the Museum of American History. Other galleries and museums associated with the Smithsonian are located in nearby historic buildings. Christmas is everywhere in sight, and at night the panoramic vista is illuminated like a magnacolor Christmas decoration.

Rising from the grassy banks of the Potomac River, a splendid Carrara marble and tinted glass tribute to artistic endeavor, the John F. Kennedy Center for the Performing Arts plays host to a mind-boggling array of talent. At Christmas, the Concert Hall, Eisenhower Theater, American Film Institute Theater, Terrace Theater, Opera House, and the necessary supporting amenities honor various performers.

The Kennedy Center Holiday Festival requires eight legal-sized pages to announce December's schedule. In 1971, the year the Kennedy Center opened, an anonymous benefactor made it possible for the center to invite tourists and Washingtonians alike to attend free holiday programs in the Grand Foyer and Concert Hall. The first festival included a *Messiah* sing-along, the D.C. Youth Orchestra, several choirs, and handbell ringers. In 1982 the Kennedy Center Holiday Festival had some 60 events with hundreds of performers taking part. Each year, corporate sponsors, unions, the recording industry, federal agencies, and individuals support the festival. The festival strives to fulfill its role as a forum for *all* people by providing performances free to the public, programs of cultural and racial diversity both in the performance and historical sense. It also provides a stage for performing groups of high quality who would otherwise not be able to present their programs in the nation's cultural center.

There is simply a staggering number of Washington events to consid-

Photos: Smithsonian National Museum of American History, John F. Kennedy Center for the Performing Arts, National Cathedral.

er, and happily, personal preference is more important than pocketbook. You might attend the classic and delightful *Nutcracker* performed by the Washington Ballet at the Lisner Auditorium. The National Symphony brings music to life in the two-century-old *Messiah* oratorio in the Kennedy Center Concert Hall; the jammed and wonderful sing-along *Messiah,* also at the Kennedy Center, is a participatory marvel! *A Christmas Carol* plays at the Ford Theater to happy crowds, while the Folger Theater hosts *A Medieval Christmas Pageant.* The DAR Constitution Hall rings with a Christmas concert by The United States Air Force Band. And at the annual Tuba Christmas gathering on the Ellipse in mid-December, 500 local professional and amateur musicians join their tubas, sousaphones, and baritone horns to delight strollers half a mile away with Christmas songs.

Many historic homes herald the Christmas season by welcoming folks to join them in candlelight tours. Woodlawn Plantation, Mount Vernon, is decorated with boxwood wreaths, pine cone swags, and kissing balls. The dining table is set as it might have been in the days of Nellie Custis, who lived in the house in the early 1800s. Right downtown, the Logan Circle Victorian Christmas house tour features nine homes decorated in the Victorian style, as is the neighborhood, with garlands and ribbons hung on the street lamps. Horses and buggies are used for transport between homes. The Woodrow Wilson house is right near the center of town. Montpelier Mansion in suburban Maryland opens the 18th century Georgian home and boxwood gardens once belonging to Major Thomas Snowden and his wife, Ann. Belle Grove Plantation is decorated with natural materials 18th century style, and includes grapevine wreaths decorated with bittersweet and milkweed pods.

National leaders change, parties in power come and go, new buildings sprout and historic buildings enjoy rejuvenation, but the traditions don't seem to change very much or very fast. Along about noon on the day before Christmas a sense of purpose

seems to overtake Washington; you see it in people's faces. It is a good and welcome sight. People have last minute things to accomplish: someone to see before tomorrow or an errand to run. Or, maybe, they're just thinking it hasn't been such a bad year after all. But as dusk creeps in to announce Christmas Eve and the lights begin to twinkle and the candles are lit, the strain and busyness melts into smiles and friendliness and comradery. Throughout Washington, music is heard, bells are rung, and children's voices penetrate the night air. Even as streets grow quieter, this time seems to draw participation from everyone. For those unable to enjoy a hearth and the warmth of friends or family this Christmas Eve, there are well over a thousand congregations in the Washington area celebrating the birth of Christ who welcome others to share in their joy.

In Georgetown, Holy Trinity Church celebrates the eucharist. The National Presbyterian Church celebrates as well. The national Cathedral has three major events: the family service and Christmas pageant, the carillon recital, and an organ prelude and festival eucharist. Grace Lutheran Church has an hour-long candlelight service at eleven.

To the visitor, Washington is a lot like any other American town. There really aren't any streets where the sky is blocked out; the shops are mostly small and inviting; and the Christmas decorations are as individual as the names above the doors. The same representative Santas ring bells, the vendors and hucksters are not out of proportion, and even the "bag people" take time Christmas Day to watch the skaters on the iced-over pools on the Mall. The strings and strings of lights placed by the National Park Service to decorate even the shrubbery throughout the city create a subtle background for the many Christmas activities. The homeless are sheltered, the hungry fed, the children cared for by various civic and governmental groups, by churches and synagogues and mosques, and even by the individual on the street, caught up in the whole panoply of Christmas.

The nation's capital is an American birthright. Christmas is truly a wonderful time to be here.

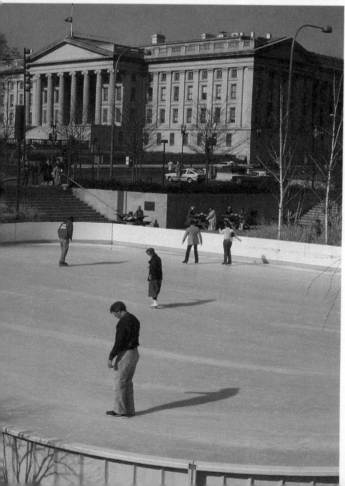

Photos: Georgetown Park Mall, singers at the Mazza Gallerie, ice skaters in Pershing Park near the Treasury Department.

The Shepherd's Tale

A simple tale it was, how deep one night
While palms rose up above our sleeping flock
Like graceful fingers pointing to the sky,
There, of a sudden, voices rose and grew
Across our hearing, till we thought
The vault of heaven had retuned its spheres.
(Or so at least did Jonathan describe
That heavenly music in the learned way
His schooling in the town had tutored him.)
But I anticipate my story: mark me well,
The melodies at first seemed like a breeze,
They cooled and soothed our hearing.
None did dare to tell another—such a charm
To hear those voices carol—for we feared
One word from us would still those glorious throats.
And so we lay and listened, while our sheep,
Their bodies breathing softly in the night,
Seemed also to enjoy that wondrous sound
Which fell in waves across our hillside cove.
I cannot tell it rightly; even Jonathan,
With all his Greek and Latin, found no words
To picture chimes that spoke such accents rare.
But then another wonder joined the first:
Unblemished light that fell from heaven above

Like sunbeams sifting slowly down a well.
Within that tower of light a ladder grew,
Like Jacob's in the scriptures; there they glowed,
Like candles spreading radiance through the dark,
With faces shining like none ever seen.
And then the music parted. (It was they who played,
Their voices, rather, that like instruments,
Had made the music that so held us thrall.)
And now we heard their words—such words they were!
That heaven's door ajar,
A child had come to lead us through the night
To where his otherworldly dwelling stood,
So that we might in glory join him there.
The words took fire and set our souls aglow.
Like children tempted by a regal feast,
We left our sheep for shadowy Bethlehem.
But I for one looked back: a wondrous sight!
To see those radiant beings on that stair,
And as I stared, they slowly disappeared
Into the deeper darkness; stars once more
Enveloped heaven with their tinseled glow.
Messiah named, we found him in his crib,
A shepherd who would lead his flock, like us,
Until bright morning opened wide the day.

The Christmas Tree

LUCENA J. KIBBE

Otis Bisbe was looking through the window of the log house, watching his sister Electa; or, Lecty, as they called her. He wished he could be out there with her playing in the snow. He couldn't though because he had no boots, and Ma said his feet would get soaked even if she could still pull his outgrown shoes over his feet. He wished he had boots like Orson did, but Orson went to school and even helped Pa with chores so he had to have them. Otis didn't. Suddenly he saw a movement at the crest of the hill.

"Orson's coming, Ma," he announced as his brother's head appeared over the rise behind the barn.

"All right," Zilpha answered and reached for the quilt she had laid handy on the rocker. She had promised that when Orson came home from school she would wrap Otis up, feet and all, in the quilt. Then he could ride on the sled with the others.

Zilpha put Otis, well bundled up, on the front of the sled that Burr had made for

the children. Electa clambered on behind.

"I'll just pull them up by the barn, and we'll ride down the little hill toward Grandma's," Orson assured her.

"Yes. Don't take them on the big hill toward the schoolhouse," Zilpha cautioned. "They're too small."

"Otis is; he's only three. But I'm not; I'm seven," Lecty argued.

"No big hill," Zilpha repeated, and the matter was settled.

They didn't stay out long, for choretime came early and Orson was expected to help. Otis' face was rosy when he emerged from his quilt, but his body was warm to Zilpha's touch. Lecty's thin one shivered from the cold as she held out red hands toward the open hearth of the stove.

"My mittens are wearing out. Besides they're too small," she complained.

When Burr and Orson came in from the barn, the family sat down to a supper of bread and milk and applesauce. Heads bowed as Burr asked God's blessing on them all.

Orson lifted his light curly head as soon as the amen was said and made his big announcement. He had waited till they were all together.

"We're to have a Christmas tree down to school. Teacher told us. Not just the pupils, but all the folks around. There'll be pieces to speak and a real tree decorated with popcorn and pine cones and apples and maybe even cranberries. May . . . may we go, Ma?"

His question pleaded for permission. He had even been careful to say "may" and not "can" so Ma wouldn't be distracted by an error in grammar. Both Burr and Zilpha had stopped eating as soon as he mentioned Christmas, and he realized that their too great attention suggested displeasure.

The year was 1879; the place was upstate New York. Christmas was little noted there at that time and certainly not celebrated as a holiday. Many local people were descendants of settlers from Massachusetts where Christmas was not declared a legal holiday until 1856, some time after their parents had left. The Puritans had wanted to rid themselves of the excesses of revelry and drunkenness that often marked Christmas in 17th century England. To other parents besides the Bisbes it would seem a strange and perhaps sinful reversal of custom.

"I don't know," Zilpha told Orson honestly. "A Christmas tree sounds pagan to me."

"But, Ma. . . ."

"Your father and I will discuss it and decide." Her voice was gentle, and with that he had to be content.

Otis heard the discussion that night, though he didn't understand it. The older children had gone to bed up in the loft, one on each side of the ladder. Otis in the trundle bed had not yet gone to sleep.

"What will we do about this Christmas tree?" Burr's face was serious in the lamplight as he sat at the table peeling and eating small russet apples. He hated to disappoint his children.

"It's hard to know." Zilpha was sitting in the kitchen rocker out of range of the light of the lamp, for her weak eyes were sensitive to artificial light. "It certainly isn't the way our folks felt things should be done. Why, I remember when Pa was church clerk and he read us the old minutes of the church. It was noted that some of the sister churches were falling into the heresy of celebrating a day called Christmas. So they set the date for their annual business meeting for December 25 each year to avoid the falling away by their own members. Pa approved that action."

"I know. I know. I don't think I'd go that far, though. And the children would be disappointed now that they've heard about it."

"I don't like to see them saddened either. But if they must be for their own good, a few tears now are better than spiritual downfall later."

Zilpha always put her children's welfare above their happiness.

"But will it hurt them? As I got it from Orson, the teacher just had in mind to bring a tree into the school and decorate it a little and then have the children speak pieces."

Zilpha thought for a while before asking, "Isn't this the Sunday Elder Baker plans to speak at the church?"

Burr nodded. The local church had no resident minister, but whenever a preacher was available they had services. Of late, Elder Baker had come most frequently.

"Perhaps we can discuss it with him then."

"That's a good idea," agreed Burr. "Tomorrow is Saturday, and I'd planned to go down to Mr. Allen's on business. I'll mention it to him. If the teacher stays over this weekend, he'll be at church. We can get his view too."

The children heard nothing from their parents about the Christmas tree the next day or Sunday morning as they got ready for church. They knew better than to ask. If they teased, the answer would certainly be no. They also knew that they would be told when a decision was reached.

After the Sunday church service, all the children met in a small anteroom for Sunday school. The adults gathered in the back pews, but instead of the usual Bible study they discussed the proposed celebration.

The teacher apologized for telling the children the plans before consulting anyone. He had assumed there would be some kind of party and had been amazed at the excitement of the pupils and the disapproval of the parents. He had been brought up in a city and, new teaching certificate in hand, had started his first teaching job in this rural area.

Several parents asked exactly what he proposed. Others expressed their feeling that this sort of thing had never been done here before and had been strongly frowned on by their fathers and mothers.

Elder Baker, a tall man with bushy white hair and piercing blue eyes, understood the concern of the parents not to mislead their children. He agreed that no one knew the exact date of Christ's birth, but pointed out that the Bible told of the event at length. He explained that the objection to it had been the way it was dishonored by people's behavior. Since there surely would be no drunkenness or rowdiness at the schoolhouse, he concluded by saying he saw no harm in celebrating Jesus' birth.

The teacher assured them that the biblical account of the event would be given at the exercises and, further, asked the elder if he could be present and speak a few words. He agreed. Since that seemed to settle the question, Mrs. Allen, who also had been raised in town, suggested that the parents supply a gift for each of their own children.

On the way home from church Burr told Orson he might plan on the Christmas tree. Orson's long face, so like his father's, broke into a wide grin. Lecty bounced up and down,

"Goody, goody!" she exclaimed. "What's a Christmas tree?"

In the laughter that followed no one answered her, but later Orson was glad to expound on its wonders.

That night after the children were asleep, Zilpha told Burr there would be no difficulty in deciding on gifts for the children. Orson needed a new reader; Otis must have boots; and Mother Bisbe was planning to knit some mittens for Lecty.

Next afternoon Lecty was sent on an errand to Grandma's. She lived in the other log house that Burr had built as his mother asked—nearby, but far enough away so she wouldn't hear the babies cry. Otis had gone with Lecty on such errands ever since he could walk, but he didn't even ask this time. He knew he couldn't go out. No boots. While he stood at the window watching for her to come home, he saw Pa and Mr. Allen drag out of the woods a beautiful pine tree so big it didn't seem possible

and Otis wore his kilted boy's dress that was kept for church. On weekdays he had to wear Lecty's old dresses, which he hated. People would think he was a girl!

Burr hitched Old Fan to the sleigh. Orson and Electa sat with Grandpa Bisbe on a board seat put in the back of the sleigh for such occasions. Grandma Bisbe, Burr, and Zilpha rode on the seat. Otis tried to get in back, but his mother said he was still a baby and must ride in her lap. He didn't object strenuously. All that mattered tonight was the Christmas tree. It was cold but clear that night, and the moon and stars high above were bright.

it would fit in the school. He began to share the excitement Lecty had been showing ever since hearing about the tree. Orson had said a Christmas tree would be like the last day exercises Lecty had visited when Ma was teaching, with the added fun of presents. Out of hearing of their parents, Orson had told them that Santa Claus would leave gifts on the tree for them. The days seemed to drag until the party.

When the day finally came, not only did Otis have to take a long nap, but even Electa had to sleep in the afternoon. Then, when Orson got home from school, chores and supper were hurried through. Orson put on his Sunday suit. Zilpha helped Electa into her good blue dress,

White snow lay all around with splotches of dark shadow cast by trees and the sleigh.

It was two miles around by the road to the school. It took Fan but a few minutes to pull them there.

Once inside the well-filled building, Otis climbed again into Zilpha's lap. Even Electa sat on Burr's lap in order to see better. Orson sat with the other school children in the front seats.

The teacher's desk had been moved to one side to make room for the tree. It went up, up, up, to the very beams of the roof. It was decorated with polished apples, strings of popcorn and cranberries. There were even a few strands of tinsel. On it and beneath it were presents.

To Otis, there seemed to be a great many, certainly more than he had ever seen in his three short years.

"Look," Lecty whispered to him. "Look up high. There's a pair of red mittens!"

Otis nodded, but he was too engrossed in the whole beautiful tree to worry about red mittens.

The school children had never seen anything like this before, either. They only took their eyes from the tree when the exercises began and they had to speak their pieces. Since they memorized something to speak in school each Friday as well as longer and more involved selections for the final day of school, they spoke loudly and, in general, very well. Otis never heard a word. His full attention was diverted to the tree, taking in each detail.

After all the pupils had taken their turn, Elder Baker gave a sermon. It was much shorter than his Sunday messages, being only a half hour long.

Then the teacher rose, saying the presents now would be given out. He had everyone's attention, even Otis' and Electa's.

First, the names of the school boys of the winter term were called. Otis watched as Orson got a book. Then the girls and younger boys who had attended summer term were called one by one to receive their presents.

"I wonder if we'll get some, too," Lecty whispered to Otis, "even if we don't go to school."

Otis wasn't too concerned. Just the tree was enough right now. However, when almost at the end the teacher called, "Electa and Otis Bisbe," he clambered down quickly and took Lecty's hand. Down the short aisle they walked, the slender, pig-tailed little girl with arms like broomsticks and the sturdy, solemn, dark-haired boy, whose toddle had just become a walk.

The teacher reached way up and took down from the tree the pair of red mittens and handed them to the delighted Electa. Then he reached under the tree, picked up a pair of small copper-toed boots and, turning, held them out to Otis. With a glad cry the boy let loose of his sister's hand and ran for the boots. Clutching them in his arms, he smiled widely at the teacher. Now he could play out in the snow! Electa herded him back to their seat, but she couldn't take his hand. Both hands were clasped around those boots.

Otis held them up to his mother as soon as he reached her. "Put them on," he begged.

She complied. Taking off the tight shoes into which she had managed to squeeze his feet, she put the new boots with the copper toes on Otis. He sat looking at them during the remaining few minutes that they were there. He had never seen anything so pretty in his life.

Otis went to sleep on the way home and was laid fully dressed on the trundle bed while Zilpha helped a happy but tired Electa to bed. When she came down from the loft and started undressing Otis, however, she ran into a problem. Every time she started to pull off a boot he would wake up just enough to say, "No."

"Looks as if," Burr told her genially from where he and Orson sat by the stove, "looks as if you might have to let him sleep in them tonight."

Orson giggled.

"No." Zilpha disagreed forcefully. "They're not going to say about any man of mine, old or young, that he goes to bed with his boots on!" (The country expression was used of someone so lazy or senile that he must be told every move to make.)

With that, she quickly and deftly pulled off a boot and had it in Otis' hands almost before he missed it. The other came off just as fast. Otis slept with them clasped tightly in his arms.

Next morning Otis was out early making tracks in the snow with his new boots while he waited for Lecty. They were to go to Grandma's, but Lecty wasn't ready yet. Otis didn't mind. He was in no hurry. When she finally came out, Lecty looked excited.

"I found out," she told him. "I found out. Remember Orson kept saying Santa Claus would bring the presents? Well, he did bring my mittens because I just asked Ma if she had ever seen the yarn in my mittens before last night. She said no, and you know Ma wouldn't lie."

Otis nodded, not quite understanding. To him, as yet, things he needed just came from somewhere. He didn't know. He was just glad he had those boots.

"I could have asked about your boots," she added, "but somehow I didn't think I should."

Electa never forgot that Christmas tree. Otis, being so young, might have, had she let him. But she talked about the Christmas tree and insisted they play Christmas tree for so long that it was woven into his memory, too. Indeed, at age 80 they still reminisced about those red mittens and the wonderful copper-toed boots.

Colonial Yuletide

CORINNE MADDEN ROSS

Can you imagine Christmas without a Christmas tree? In America today that would be unthinkable! Yet back in the colonial era, that beloved symbol of the holiday season was virtually unknown. The charming custom of decorating a fir tree with glittering baubles and flickering candles did not become popular in this country until the mid-1800s.

Despite the lack of Christmas trees, however, the courageous men, women, and children who came to colonize America in the 1600s and 1700s managed to observe Christmas in the New World in a colorful variety of ways.

The 13 original colonies stretched along the East Coast from Massachusetts (which then included Maine) to Georgia. Most of the early settlers were English, but the colonists also included people from Scotland, Ireland, Germany, Holland, France, and Sweden. Although they brought many of the holiday traditions of their homelands with them when they came, Christmas in the colonies often turned out to be very different from anything they had known in the past.

Let's take a journey back in time to America's colonial days and share in some of those long-ago holiday observances. We will begin in the South at Jamestown, Virginia, which is generally believed to be the site of the first Christmas celebration by English settlers in the New World.

Jamestown was settled in 1607, but the colonists had little to celebrate during their first few years in America. More than half of their original number died from starvation and sickness, and the rest barely managed to survive. Their earliest Christmas observances were limited to gathering for a sermon and praying for the arrival of fresh supplies. Hostile Indians added to the Jamestowners' miseries. Then their leader, Captain John Smith, was captured by Indians, only to be saved from death by Chief Powhatan's daughter, Pocahontas. After that relations between the Indians and colonists began to improve. The Indians even invited the Jamestown folk to feast with them on Christmas Day.

The occasion was a welcome respite from the colonists' harsh existence, and the dreadful weather gave them even more reason to appreciate the cozy warmth of the Indian lodges. Captain Smith recorded the event in his journal, mentioning "the extreme winde, rayne, frost and snow" and adding, "We were never more merrie nor fedde on more plentie of good Oysters, Fish, Flesh, Wild fowle and good Breade; nor never had we better fires in England than in the warm smokie houses."

In 1610 ships carrying new settlers as well as the desperately needed supplies arrived, and the Jamestown colony finally began to grow. Ten years later its population had increased to 4000, and by 1648 the colony had 15,000 inhabitants. Life for the settlers became progressively easier, despite renewed Indian attacks and difficulties with the English crown. The tobacco industry, which started in 1612, prospered with the establishment of great plantations in the country beyond the town. Other settlers forged farther westward, where they wrested small farms from the wilderness.

In 1699 the colonial government moved to nearby Williamsburg, and Jamestown was virtually abandoned. The new capital soon became the center of Virginia's political, cultural, and social life. By the mid-1700s the small town of Williamsburg had grown into a colonial city of gracious demeanor and fine houses, including the handsome Governor's Palace. Williamsburg's Christmas season was observed with an elegance and gaiety unmatched by any other of the original colonies.

Inns and houses were filled to bursting with holiday guests. Bruton Parish Church was decorated with pine garlands, holly, and bayberry candles; shop windows received wreaths of pine. Williamsburg residents adorned their Christmas tables with magnificent arrangements of fruit, nuts, greenery, pinecones, and other natural delights. At night candles glowed in every window, and huge bonfires made festive beacons announcing that Christmas had arrived. Gentlemen in fine attire danced with equally resplendent ladies at grand balls to the music of fiddlers. Fox hunts and games of dice or draughts were popular amusements. Christmas was also a time for visiting friends and for feasting.

The holiday season in the surrounding Virginia countryside was even merrier, if possible, than in Williamsburg. The wealthy plantation owners believed in celebrating Christmas with all the joyous traditions of Old England. Their hospitality was limitless. Country squires and their families held open house for all comers.

Carriages overflowing with guests would descend on the plantations in the weeks and days before Christmas. Other visitors would ride up on horseback. All were made welcome to stay for dinner, for the night, or even for a month! No invitations were required. Friends and relatives, and strangers too, arrived and left as they pleased. A British magazine of the time described Virginian hospitality in glowing terms: ". . . full tables and open doors . . . strangers are fought after with greediness as they pass the country, to be invited."

Entertainment was lavish and continuous. During the daytime the men hunted or rode to the hounds. Guests also boated, held races and other sporting events, and played games. At night there were music, dancing, more games, and, of course, vast amounts of food to eat. The parties often lasted till the morning.

Each plantation house was beautifully decorated with Christmas greens. Red-berried holly and boughs of fir were brought in from the woods to festoon doors, hallways, living rooms, and ballrooms. Greenery was draped over mirrors, mantels, and pictures. Mistletoe was also much in favor as a decoration, and the men of the

by a great blast of noise. The countryside resounded with exploding firecrackers and the roar of many muskets being fired into the air. Although sometimes thought to be an American addition to the South's version of an English Christmas, the custom of making noise during the holidays was practiced in some parts of England in pre-Christian times. The custom derived from the belief that making a racket would frighten off evil spirits.

household were sent off to gather armloads of the waxy-leaved branches with their pale white berries. Mistletoe, believed by the ancient Druids to have mysterious powers, was not easy to acquire. It was usually to be found growing on the very highest boughs of a tree. Sometimes the men would climb the tree to cut it, but often they simply shot it down.

Christmas in Virginia also included the Old World custom of the Yule log. It was the servants' chore to search the woods for a proper tree, usually an immense oak. It was then cut down and the giant log hauled back to the house where it was set afire on the hearth. The servants enjoyed the task and made every effort to find the largest tree possible—for an excellent reason. On many plantations, the servants were freed from work for as long as the Yule log burned. In some instances, they would even soak the log with water so that it would burn longer! Everyone in the household knew of the scheme, of course, and it was the cause of much secret merriment.

Christmas morning on the plantations was announced

Nowadays on Christmas mornings, most families spend hours unwrapping mountains of presents. But in colonial days, gift-giving was usually limited to a few toys for the children—perhaps from Father Christmas, the old British spirit of Yuletide. The servants, too, were presented with small gifts—clothing, candies, and trinkets. Later on in the morning, families and their guests attended church services, if there was a church nearby.

The major event of the day, however, was Christmas dinner, served in midafternoon and lasting for hours. Preparations for the feast would have been underway for weeks. The mistresses of plantation households kept close supervision over their servants as they stewed, roasted, and baked. Tempting odors wafted from every kitchen, giving rise to the old Virginia saying that claimed, "Even if you were to lose all of your senses except that of smell, you would still know when it was Christmas!"

The holiday dinner consisted of a lengthy series of courses beginning with, perhaps, a tureen of turtle soup, followed by oysters and other seafood, venison, roast beef with Yorkshire pudding, suckling pig and boiled mutton, hickory-smoked ham and roast turkey, wild duck, partridge, or goose. An array of vegetable dishes accompanied the meats, plus platters of hot biscuits and corn bread. Jams, jellies, brandied peaches, and other condiments also appeared in profusion. Desserts included fruitcakes and rich layer cakes, plum pudding, a selection of pies and tarts, almond cookies, molded jellies, and fruit. In addition to all of this, dishes of candy, raisins, and nuts were set out for munching.

The other southern colonies—Maryland, North and South Carolina, and Georgia—were also settled mainly by the British. Their Christmas celebrations during the colonial period were, like Virginia's, mostly southern adaptations of old English traditions.

Farther north, in the middle colonies of New York, New Jersey, Pennsylvania, and Delaware, Christmas was observed in a very different manner. The middle colonies' earliest holiday customs came, along with their settlers, from Sweden and Holland. The English came somewhat later, and in the 1700s German and Scotch-Irish settlers found their way to the region.

The Dutch arrived first, in the early 1600s. They named the territory New Netherland and around 1613 established trading posts on Manhattan Island (which they called New Amsterdam), near present-day Albany, and along the Delaware River. Then in 1638 a group of Swedish colonists came to the New World. The Swedes built several settlements along the Delaware River not far from the Dutch and called the region New Sweden. The Dutch deeply resented the Swedish encroachments and in 1655 seized control. Nine years later, the British stepped in and took over the entire territory.

For those early Swedish settlers, Christmas in the New World was probably a solemn one at first. Little is known about their colonial holiday observances, but certainly many managed to concoct a cheering bowl of *glögg*, a hot spicy brew, to commemorate the day. The Swedes and, in later years, the Germans and English welcomed in the New Year with mumming. The Swedes called it Fantasticals. Bands of masked, costumed men paraded in the streets and went from house to house acting out short plays or reciting verses. In return the revelers were offered coins or something to eat or drink.

The Dutch from the very start celebrated Christmas in America with great gusto. They were a hearty lot who thoroughly enjoyed good food and good times. Christmas was one of their favorite holidays. Even their earliest Christmases in New Netherland were jolly ones with bonfires, games and sports, sleigh rides, and dancing. In 1625 the Dutch colonists in New Amsterdam dined on wild turkey, lit a Yule log, and went ice skating.

The name day of the colony's patron saint, St. Nicholas, was on December 6 and marked the start of the Christmas season. The city fathers decreed that all business would be suspended from St. Nicholas Eve to Twelfth Night, January 6.

Colonial Dutch children were given their presents on St. Nicholas Day. The youngsters believed that St. Nick came all the way from Holland each year. It was supposed that he sailed on the *Christmas Ship*, which would dock sometime in early December, laden with toys, books, cakes, and fruit. From New Amsterdam the vessel made its way up the Hudson to Albany. Excited children all along the route waited impatiently for it to arrive.

Once on dry land, St. Nicholas made his rounds riding on a white horse. A servant named Knecht Ruprecht accompanied him carrying an open sack. On St. Nicholas Eve, a knock would come at the door and in would stride the tall, bearded saint (represented by a relative or family friend) wearing bishop's robes and carrying a miter. Kindly St. Nick then presented the youngsters with their gifts; but Knecht Ruprecht was not so agreeable a visitor. Waving a fistful of switches, he would threaten to carry off any misbehaving boys or girls in his large sack to the children's mingled fear and delight!

The Dutch name for St. Nicholas was *SinterKlaas*. Although almost every group of colonists brought its own Old World version of St. Nicholas to America, it was the Dutch *SinterKlaas* who was later, in the 1800s, transformed into Santa Claus.

English Quakers came to the middle colonies in the late 1600s, settling in Philadelphia. Unlike the southern colonists from England or the English and Dutch in New York, the Quakers considered keeping holidays "vain." For them Christmas was just another day. They did, however, share with their fellow English an appreciation of food and drink, neither of which was forbidden by their faith. In 1754 a visitor to Philadelphia reported seeing a bowl of punch so enormous it could have "swimm'd half a dozen young geese!"

In the 1700s German colonists from the Rhine provinces emigrated to America. Many settled in the western part of Pennsylvania where they became known as Pennsylvania Dutch. This mix-up of terms resulted from other settlers mistaking the word *deutsch* (which means "German") for Dutch.

Like the Dutch, the German settlers celebrated Christmas with festive parties, games, and sports. They enjoyed shooting contests, mumming, greased pig races, and fireworks. Pennsylvania Dutch housewives prepared mountains of food for the holidays, including the traditional spicy German cookie called *lebkuchen*. The cookies were baked in ornate molds the shapes of animals, stars, hearts, men on horseback, and even Indians wielding hatchets. A great many cookies were needed. In addition to those eaten by the family, some were given to the poor, and others were used for window decorations. Still more were put aside for *Pelznichol*, the Pennsylvania Dutch name for the German *Belsnickle*.

KristKindlein, the Christ child, visited German children on Christmas Eve bearing presents. *Pelznichol*, too, brought presents. But he also was known to punish youngsters who had been wicked. He would announce his presence by making scary faces through a window. Then he would come banging his way into the house where he would fiercely question the children (and their parents) as to whether the young ones had been bad or good. Well-behaved youngsters received candies and small gifts; those who had misbehaved got only a switch. But, most likely, the unlucky ones were just as rare then as they are now. It would take a stern parent indeed to tell tales on a small, wide-eyed son or daughter. And Christmastime always seems to bring out the most angelic behavior in even the most mischievous child!

Another group of settlers to arrive in the mid-1700s were the Moravians. Originally from a region in old Czechoslovakia known as Moravia, they had fled from their homeland to Germany in order to escape religious persecution. A German count, Nikolaus von Zinzendorf, offered them refuge on his estate. He later led some of them to Savannah, Georgia, and to Pennsylvania. Another group founded Salem (now Winston-Salem) in North Carolina. The Pennsylvania Moravians settled the towns of Bethlehem and Nazareth.

Christmas for the Moravians was very much a religious holiday, but not at all a solemn one. They believed in worshiping God with music, the lighting of candles, and good, simple food. On Christmas Eve these components were combined into the Moravian "love feast," a vigil service during which the congregation lit candles and shared sugar buns and mugs of coffee as the choir sang.

In 1754 the voices of the chorus were augmented by the Moravians' first trombone choir. A year later, according to legend, the brass choir was said to have saved the Bethlehem settlement from an Indian raid. It was the musicians' custom to climb to the church belfry at dawn on Christmas Day to announce the birth of Christ with "merry music." On that morning in 1755, hostile Indians were hiding in the woods surrounding the town. They planned to attack at dawn, but just as they were about to surge forward the trombone choir blared forth. The Indians, believing the noise to be a warning from the Great Spirit, scattered in terror!

Another Moravian Christmas tradition was the *putz*, or nativity scene. Their version of the beloved Christmas story was delightfully extensive and involved a great deal of preparation. Masses of moss and greenery were gathered for decoration; snow-covered hills and valleys were constructed; and a backdrop was painted with a moon, stars, and, perhaps, a few clouds.

The *putz* differed according to each family's taste. A variety of biblical tableaux was included in addition to the manger scene itself. Small carved wooden figures represented Joseph, Mary, and the Babe, shepherds, the three Wise Men, and villagers going about their chores. There were figures of animals, too—cows, donkeys, sheep, rabbits, and sometimes even wolves or mountain lions. Overhead a host of angels hovered. Beeswax candles lighted up the charming scene.

A traveler visiting New England at Christmastime today will find the region abounding with holiday festivities. Christmas trees twinkle with colored lights on every village green; candles gleam in the windows of wreath-bedecked 18th and 19th century houses; white, steepled churches resound with the strains of traditional carols. From quaint old seaports to the tiniest mountain hamlets, the season is ushered in with great joy. During most of New England's colonial era, however, none of these signs of Christmas were present. Not only were there no decorated trees or carol singing, but Christmas itself also was actually banned for many of the early colonial years. In fact, December 25 was not considered a day of celebration for most New Englanders for almost three centuries!

The first permanent settlers in the region were English Puritans, who arrived at Plymouth, Massachusetts, in 1620. They were members of a group of Protestants who bitterly opposed the ways of the established Church of England, including its manner of celebrating holidays—particularly Christmas. Unlike most of the English who came to colonize other regions of the New World, the Massachusetts Puritans despised what they felt were ungodly, rowdy Christmas practices.

The Puritans' first Christmas in America was grim—cold, rainy, and wet—and almost went completely unobserved. For the colonists it was just another workday. Governor William Bradford noted in his journal that the first house for common use was erected in December "on the 25th day," not mentioning that the date was Christmas. The only festive touch was contributed by the captain of the *Mayflower*, who was not a Puritan. Captain Jones generously shared a portion of his own ration with those whose provisions had run out.

The first Thanksgiving feast was held in the Plymouth colony the following year. But Christmas once again was ignored by the Puritans. The original colonists, however, had by then been joined by a few shiploads of new settlers, and not all of them held to the same stern beliefs. Governor Bradford wrote that "on the day called Christmas" he had been forced to admonish some of the men for not working. They told him, he noted, that it went against their conscience to labor on that day. A reason-able man, the governor let it pass and, attempting to set a good example, led his own flock off to work.

Later that day Bradford came upon the rebels once again. This time they were enjoying a game of ball! He took the ball away and told the sinners that what they were doing—playing while others worked—was against *his* conscience. And if they insisted on keeping Christmas as a matter of faith, they should do so in their homes, but "there should be no gaming or revelry in the streets."

Back in England, the Protestant movement grew in power and in 1642 the celebration of Christmas was totally banned. The General Court of Massachusetts followed suit in 1659, enacting a stringent law that read: "Whoever shall be found observing any such day as Christmas or the like, either by forebearance of labor or feasting, or in any other way as a festival shall be fined five shillings." The ruling explicitly forbade dancing, card playing, all musical instruments except the drum, trumpet, and jews-harp, and even mince pie!

It may seem odd to ban such an innocent feature of Christmas as a pie. But mince pies in the old days were often baked in an oval shape resembling a manger, sometimes with a tiny figure of the Christ child placed on top. The Puritans looked upon the custom as sacrilegious, a hated form of idol worship. Carol singing was also frowned upon, as was the English custom of decorating churches with evergreens and holly.

In England, Christmas began to be observed once more when Charles II was restored to the throne in 1660. In Massachusetts, the law banning holiday celebrations was repealed in 1681. Five years later the royal governor held Christmas services in Boston's Town House, which is thought to be the first legal observance of the holiday in Massachusetts. And throughout New England congregations other than Puritan began to erect their own churches, where Christmas was celebrated with music, candles, and once-forbidden boughs of fir.

But the gradual spread of these festive holiday practices greatly dismayed many of the still Puritanical ministers of the 1700s, including the fiery Cotton Mather. In his view the English manner of keeping Christmas was "Bacchanallian," marked with such disgraceful observances as "an excess of wine" and "mad mirth." In 1711 Mather felt the need to reprimand even some of his own congregation. For he had heard, undoubtedly with horror, that "a number of people of both sexes, belonging many of them to my flock, have had on the Christmas night this past week a Frolick, a revelling feast, and a Ball, which discovers their corruption!"

Eventually, the vigilant opposition to Christmas in New England began to fade. Another century and a half had to pass, however, before December 25 was named a legal holiday in Massachusetts in 1858! And it was not until the early 1900s that New England finally began to celebrate Christmas openly.

Today we celebrate Christmas with a colorful blend of traditions brought by our colonial ancestors to the New World. An evergreen tree sparkles in nearly every home. Houses are dressed with pine boughs, holly, and mistletoe after the English fashion. Carols sung by candlelight reflect the joy of a Moravian love feast. And, finally, the giving spirit of the Dutch St. Nicholas reminds us of God's best gift, his Son.

Christmas Corners

A Legacy of Love

The Carols of Alfred S. Burt

ANNE S. BURT

On the pine-covered shores of Lake Superior in the upper peninsula of Michigan nestles the small town of Marquette. It sits in a wonderland of natural beauty with vast virgin forests, streams, rock formations, and wild floral foliage. Winter places a deep blanket of snow over the countryside; but spring bursts out, bringing new life and an array of color. Here on April 22, 1920, the composer, Alfred Shaddick Burt, was born.

Alfred's arrival at the rectory next to St. Paul's Episcopal Church on High Street was heralded by his father, the Reverend Bates Gilbert Burt, his mother, Emily May, a 12-year-old sister, Frances Deborah, and a two-year-old brother, John Harris. A close-knit family, active in community as well as church life, the Burts found time to enjoy their campsite on the shore of the lake in an area called Middle Island Point. A two-story frame home, christened "Furugaard," was built among the towering pines. Its picture window gave a panoramic view of the lake. No matter where the Burts traveled they would return to this spot for rest and inspiration.

In 1922 Father Burt accepted a call to the parish of All Saints' Episcopal Church in Pontiac, Michigan. For the next 25 years this industrial, manufacturing city would be home. Al grew up in the shadow of the lofty, brick tower of the church. His activities centered around the church calendar. He attended Sunday school, sang in the choir, served as an acolyte, and used the church gymnasium as his playground. It was a busy, but happy household in those formative years.

Through Father Burt's creative talents, the tradition began of sending an original carol as a Christmas card to friends and parishioners. He wrote both the music of the season and the words of faith from 1922 to 1941. The carols were as natural an expression of the Burt Christmas as the spicy tree in the rectory or Mother Burt's famous plum pudding.

As a self-taught musician, Father Burt was delighted when Al began to show an interest in music. When Al was 10 years of age, he received his first instrument, a "silver trumpet" (really a cornet), as a bribe to enter the local hospital for an appendectomy. He learned the fingering while recuperating. This horn would take him into bands, orchestras, and state competitions, where he would win many awards and become known as a "child prodigy." He also studied piano, but never felt it was his major instrument.

Al's first compositions were fanfares for the church festivals of Easter and Christmas. One of his most ardent admirers was the church organist, Wihla Hutson. Shar-ing the intracacies of the church pipe organ, she and Al became great musical friends. She was a guest in the rectory on many a Christmas Eve, when, after the midnight service, she was unable to travel the icy roads to her home in Detroit. A family tradition of stocking presents accompanied by an original poem introduced the Burts to her talent for verse. As "part of the family" she watched with avid interest Al's musical growth over the years.

During high school days, Al enjoyed a wide range of musical expression, but it was the new modern idiom of jazz that fascinated him the most. He formed a dance band, which was featured at church functions; and his family tolerated a set of trap drums in the rectory attic. His father discussed many times Al's feelings for this new form of music, not fully understanding his interest, but never discouraging him.

Al chose the University of Michigan School of Music in Ann Arbor for his formal education. Here he participated in the famed marching band and was the first freshman to qualify for first chair on cornet. His classical background was accomplished in the Little Symphony, the Symphony Orchestra, and the jazz expression in the dance orchestra at the Michigan Union. Graduating in 1942 with a Bachelor of Music degree, Al was chosen as an outstanding theory student. His disciplined, well-rounded foundation in musical composition would enhance his God-given abilities.

For the family card that year Al was invited by his father to write the musical setting for the carol, "O, Christmas Cometh Caroling." Father Burt had discovered the text in a small book of carols by Father Andrew, an English Catholic priest. As Al's hometown sweetheart, I was there that eventful day in November when Al's father reminded Al of the deadline for the printing of the card. Al had not yet set the lyrics to music. He asked me if I minded waiting, then went to the family Steinway and in 15 minutes wrote the music that began a father-son team.

With World War II upon us, the lyrics for the next carols were mailed to Texas, where Al was serving with the Army Air Force Band. The Christmas Eve before he left for service his "Communion Service" and an anthem, "They that Wait upon the Lord," were sung in the family church. The cards for 1943, "Jesu Parvule," and for 1944, "What Are the Signs," were reflections of the Burts' belief that Christianity, not war, was the solution to the world's problems.

Al kept busy during the war years playing with the base dance band, The Yardbirds, with the concert band, for radio broadcasts, as well as writing arrangements. He also served as a substitute trumpeter for the Houston Symphony.

During the war, I served as an operating room technician at the U.S. Naval Hospital in San Diego, California. Known as the "Singing W.A.V.E.," I divided my time between duties in surgery and entertaining with the dance band. Here I met Marine Jimmy Joyce whose original music made our hospital classic, "Leave 'Em in Stitches," a smash hit. My contact with Al was slight during the war years, but the 1944 Christmas card opened communication again. We met on a hurried leave, became engaged, and announced our plans for marriage in the fall of the following year.

On October 13, 1945, Al and I were married in All Saints' Church with Father Burt officiating. Mother Burt, ill in the hospital with cancer, was unable to attend. But we shared the festivities by taking the bridal party to her hospital room. Pinning my bridal orchid on her bedjacket, I received her blessing. She died two weeks later and was buried in the family plot in Marquette.

In 1945 the carol, "Ah, Bleak and Chill," was sent as the family card with the addition of my name. Our Christmas was spent in San Angelo, Texas, awaiting Al's discharge from the Army Air Force Band. We had honeymooned in Waukegan, Illinois, getting my discharge from the Navy.

After Al's discharge, we toured the country for 15 months with an orchestra. Many of Al's friends returned to the University of Michigan for master's degrees, but Al said he was anxious to try his professional talents in the outside world. Al wrote most of the band's arrangements, and played trumpet. We shared the spotlight together as vocalists. It was a listenable band, but had little backing and fewer bookings, so we disbanded by mutual consent.

That summer we spent time with Father Burt in Marquette. Another home had been built next to Furugaard. When completed, Dunescote would be a retirement retreat for Al's father. We shared a glorious visit filled with swimming, hiking, sailing, and reading by the light of the stone fireplace.

In the home of a dear friend, Al surprised his father by presenting the 1946 Christmas carol, having finished the music early that year. I recall the twinkle in Father Burt's eyes as he heard "All on a Christmas Morning." He had Al play it over and over, finally asking us all to

Alfred Burt at his graduation from the University of Michigan, 1942.

join in singing the words. He was Al's most devoted fan, constantly thrilled by the scope of his musical ability.

From Marquette we traveled to New York City. Al taught sightsinging, theory, and musicianship at the American Theatre Wing School. Renewing his friendship with James Wolfe, concert pianist and former college roommate, Al accepted an invitation to compose something for his upcoming concert tour. Seven concert waltzes were written in crowded quarters without a piano. The waltzes were first performed in Honolulu, Hawaii.

The carol for 1947, "Nigh Bethlehem," marked the last Christmas we would share with Father Burt. After his retirement from All Saints', he had taken a temporary rectorship near Towson, Maryland. Our holiday was filled with the favorite Burt traditions—turkey with all the trimmings, stocking presents, plum pudding, and the carol sing around the piano. Deborah Burt Norvell and her family made our holiday visit in their Towson home a lasting memory.

Early in 1948 Father Burt suffered a fatal heart attack. Once more we visited Marquette to place him beside his wife.

Returning to New York, Al and I decided we would carry on the tradition of the family card. The text for the 1948 carol was an old English rune of hospitality, given to us by the Reverend John Burt. When John was a student at the Virginia Theological Seminary, he had seen the words on a wall hanging in the Dean's office. Today, the original manuscript of "Christ in the Stranger's Guise" hangs in our home.

Al joined the Alvino Rey Orchestra in 1949; I went home to Pontiac to await our first child. It was then that Al and I decided to ask Wihla Hutson to put our ideas into poetry for the family card. Wihla and I had dinner one evening after Al had left for California. Sitting in the car outside my family's home, I babbled about the new life inside me. When Wihla asked about the text for the new carol, I naturally replied, "A lullaby!" She took these thoughts home and in the lines of "Sleep, Baby Mine" captured the feelings of motherhood we had shared.

On March 8, 1950, we used the first eight bars of this carol to announce the arrival of Diane Bates Burt. Six weeks later, we joined Al in Los Angeles. At the airport he met for the first time the one person who would rival his devotion to music.

The carols now reflected the life-style of our young

family. Working with the Alvino Rey group in the Oakland-San Francisco area, Al and I established a pattern of a secular then sacred setting for the family card. In 1950, Wihla mailed the words to "This Is Christmas," which expresses the secular joys of the season. Back in Los Angeles for Christmas 1951, we introduced the now popular "Some Children See Him," written at the same time that Wihla penned the lullaby.

Our Christmas card list had grown as we traveled from place to place from 50 to 450 names. We would drop people from the list in order to save postage only to have them write that their carol had been lost in the mail. I now understood what Father Burt had gone through to produce an original card each year.

After many years on the road, we were happy finally to be establishing roots in one place. We bought our first real home in the San Fernando Valley. I planted a trumpet vine around the front porch; Al set up a swing set for Diane; we joined a church; and Al became active in all phases of the Hollywood music world. He became assistant choir director at St. Michael and All Angels' Episcopal Church in Studio City. Then came the greatest news of all: We were expecting another baby! My world was complete!

"Come, Dear Children," the 1952 carol, was finished at the rehearsal of the Blue Reys, the singing group with Alvino Rey's Orchestra. Al asked them to sing it so that he could check the harmonies. They liked it so much they asked Al if they could add it to their performance at the annual King Family Christmas party. Al was hesitant for he didn't wish to appear pushy with his own composition. But they insisted, adding it to the familiar carols. It was the hit of the party! This was the introduction of the carols to the Hollywood musical crowd.

In 1953 our whole life would change. Al came down with a virus flu that left a lingering cough. He had been working long hours on a television show that Alvino Rey and the King Sisters were doing. Now he wished to leave town to set up the Horace Heidt Orchestra for a road tour. It was the first time I ever made a scene over his decision. He promised to return as soon as the band was polished for the show. Al was a very conscientious, dependable musical director.

I recall how tired he looked when Diane and I met him at the airport. He did not fight my call to our family internist. Entering the hospital for tests, he was still optimistic that it was a simple problem. Neither of us was prepared for the results. He had lung cancer!

On the heels of this crushing news, I lost the baby. Together, we had foreseen a struggle to establish him in the musical world, but this we had never imagined. Now our unfulfilled dreams rose to meet us. Without our deep spiritual reserve and the charm of the little girl we both loved so deeply, we could not have faced the year.

Our family and friends rallied around us. A trip to Memorial Hospital in New York City for a consultation was arranged by the Reverend Edward Miller Jr., rector of St. George's Episcopal Church and brother of Martha Miller Burt, John's wife. The hospitality offered us softened the prognosis—Al had six months to a year to live!

But later in the afternoon at a matinee of the musical comedy, *Me and Juliet,* the realization struck Al. He had long wished to write a musical. Now, revisiting the city where our young dreams had germinated, it seemed a cruel blow of fate that Al's life should end just as the brass ring was within reach. The look in Al's eyes told me we should leave. We walked, hand in hand, down the Great White Way with tears falling to wash away our frustration. No words were necessary. Fortunately, it was a city where we could be alone among the masses. But once back in the quiet of our hotel room overlooking Gramercy Park, we faced reality. It was Al's decision to return to California, to work as long as he could in the field he loved so much. His other concern was for Diane. She must have her childhood unmarred by disease. This was his final gift to her.

Back at home in the San Fernando Valley we filled

The carol, "Nigh Bethlehem," is reproduced here as it appeared on the 1947 Burt family Christmas card. © 1954 and 1957.

each day in a loving, serene atmosphere. Al's humor, warmth, compassion, and noncomplaining disposition made each day a blessing. Ours was a happy, loving family despite the tribulations. Our needs were met at every turn. A ramp for Al's wheelchair was built by the men of the church; blood was donated as transfusions became necessary; the Men's Business Club Prayer Group met at our home on Wednesday mornings so that Al could be included. My sister, Jean, left her home and husband temporarily to care for Diane.

Al gave up the trumpet first, then the piano, but his creative mind was active to the end. He went from a wheelchair to a hospital bed in our bedroom. My nursing background afforded him free nursing care. Together we worked on the music; together he and Diane shared moments to last her a lifetime; and together he and I hurried to beat the final deadline—death.

Our friends in the music business, hearing of the outcome of our trip to New York, alerted James Conkling, brother-in-law of the King Sisters and president of Columbia Records, of the urgency of Al's condition. Jim had wanted to record the carols. Now the wheels were put into motion. It gave Al a goal those last few months. Wihla was asked to write four new verses for the recording. Wihla told me that all she needed was Al's request and the words flowed so fast she could hardly write them down. "We'll Dress the House," "O, Hearken Ye," "Caroling, Caroling," and "The Star Carol" awaited music.

A volunteer chorus of the finest singers in Hollywood

The carol, "This Is Christmas," is reproduced here as it appeared on the 1950 Burt family Christmas card. © 1954 and 1957.

met in the North Hollywood Mormon Church, organized by the King Sisters, Buddy Cole, and Jimmy Joyce. Al's wheelchair could easily enter from the parking lot into the auditorium where he lead the first demonstration taping. In our home, over a cup of hot chocolate, Al reviewed the session, thrilled at the turnout for him, the lovely voices on the tape, and the fact something he had written would be released. "This is the happiest day of my life," he remarked. There was no jealousy on my part; Al's first love would always be music.

Momentum continued. Christmas 1953, we chose the triumphant hymn "O, Hearken Ye" as our family card. It was chosen as much to bolster our spirits as those of our friends and family. Al was very tired; the cobalt treatment was taking its toll. But his spirit was high!

On February 5, 1954, Al completed his final carol. Asking Jimmy Joyce to check it for him on our Steinway, Al listened carefully to the notes. Jimmy and I were enthralled with the beauty and purity of "The Star Carol." But the "Professor," as the men in the band dubbed him, perfectionist to a note, changed the tenor line in the last few bars. Then he was satisfied.

There was no denying the closeness of death. The carol was a prelude that Al knew; it was so simple in its musical character. Tired of the battle against the inevitable, Al and I shared our thoughts that last evening. He asked two things of me, to care for his music and his daughter. These promises have been kept.

His death came the next afternoon in an ambulance enroute to a hospital. Ironically, the signed contract from Columbia Records arrived by special messenger just an hour after his death. His mortal life had ended, but his musical life would begin.

On August 14, 1954, we gathered once more in Marquette. After a simple service in St. Paul's Chapel, John gave the final blessing, pouring a handful of sand taken from the beach in front of Furugaard into the grave. We had returned Al to the place where his life had begun. He was just 33 years of age. Today, three tall pine trees mark the resting place of those we placed there.

Christmas 1954, as I sat addressing the final Christmas card, "The Star Carol," I realized that I had lost not only a husband, a life-style, and a musical friend, but a Christmas card as well. The red, green, and white card was the loveliest card we had ever sent. It was signed simply, "Anne and Diane." Inside I tucked a note telling of the end of our tradition with Al's death and the release of the music for all to enjoy. Our legacy of love was our gift of music to the world that Christmas.

Since then the music of Alfred S. Burt has taken its place in the heritage of American music. It is impossible to relate the wonderful growth the carols have had. Their acceptance in concert halls, churches, schools, on radio and television, and in homes around the world truly delights our family. It was not easy those first years, hearing the familiar strains and realizing our loss; but as time has lessened our grief, we proudly face the Christmas season, knowing the carols will recall the memories of our life with the composer.

Diane, an actress-singer and musical director, finds her father in his music. Her Caroling Company in turn-of-the-century costume, sings the Burt music along with the old familiar carols. How pleased her father would be to know his daughter is following in his footsteps.

We are grateful to the many friends, known and unknown, who have kept Al's memory alive through his music. When you hear the Alfred S. Burt carols, Diane and I wish you and yours a very merry, musical Christmas and the blessing of peace and love in the New Year. For us, we will be remembering the past, keeping the words of Al's final carol in our hearts:

And when the stars in the heavens I see,
Ever and always I'll think of thee.

The secret of joy out of sorrow and gain out of loss is all there in the message of Christmas.

—*Bates G. Burt, in the 1945 Christmas card*

The Star Carol

Wihla Hutson   Alfred Burt

1. Long years a-go on a deep win-ter night,
2. Je ~ sus the Lord was that ba ~ by so small,
3. Dear ba ~ by Je ~ sus, how ti ~ ny thou art,

High in the heav'ns a star shone bright,
Laid down to sleep in a hum ~ ble stall;
I'll make a place for thee in my heart,

While in a man-ger a wee ba-by lay,
Then came the star and it stood o-ver-head,
And when the stars in the heav-ens I see,

Sweet-ly a-sleep on a bed of hay.
Shed-ding its light 'round his lit-tle bed.
Ev ~ er and al ~ ways I think of thee.

All on a Christmas Morning

Bates G. Burt — Alfred Burt

1. Oh, who are these that throng the way To Beth-le-hem, to
2. What do they has-ten thence to see In Beth-le-hem, in
3. And what is this they're car-ry-ing To Beth-le-hem, to

Beth-le-hem, And on-ward press in glad ar-ray,
Beth-le-hem, That they fare forth so mer-ri-ly,
Beth-le-hem, What is it in their arms they bring,

All on a Christ-mas morn-ing? Good Christ-tian men and
All on a Christ-mas morn-ing? Oh, they a vi-sion
All on a Christ-mas morn-ing? They bear good gifts in

maids they are From coun-tries near and lands a-far, Al-
fair would view, Would find the beau-ti-ful and true, And
rich ex-cess Of love and joy and thank-ful-ness, With

lured by yon-der beck-'ning star, All on a Christ-mas morn-ing.
faith and hope and love re-new, All on a Christ-mas morn-ing.
which man-kind they fain would bless, All on a Christ-mas morn-ing.

Al and "his friend"

Junior choir

Staff Sergeant Alfred Burt

melva

Music makers

with Alvino Rey's orchestra

Caroling, Caroling

Wihla Hutson

Alfred Burt

1. Car-ol-ing, car-ol-ing, now we go; Christ-mas bells are ring-ing! Car-ol-ing, car-ol-ing, thru the snow; Christ-mas bells are ring-ing! Joy-ous voic-es sweet and clear, Sing the sad of heart to cheer. Ding, dong, ding, dong, Christ-mas bells are ring-ing!

2. Car-ol-ing, car-ol-ing, thru the town; Christ-mas bells are ring-ing! Car-ol-ing, car-ol-ing, up and down; Christ-mas bells are ring-ing! Mark ye well the song we sing, Glad-some tid-ings now we bring. Ding, dong, ding, dong, Christ-mas bells are ring-ing!

3. Car-ol-ing, car-ol-ing, near and far; Christ-mas bells are ring-ing! Fol-low-ing, fol-low-ing, yon-der star; Christ-mas bells are ring-ing! Sing we all this hap-py morn, "Lo, the King of heav'n is born!" Ding, dong, ding, dong, Christ-mas bells are ring-ing!

Winter in

Bridal Party

Christmas

"Singing W.A. Anne Burt

melva

Some Children See Him

Wihla Hutson   Alfred Burt

1. Some chil-dren see him lil-y white, The ba-by Je-sus born this night. Some
2. Some chil-dren see him al-mond eyed, This Sav-iour whom we kneel be-side, Some
3. The chil-dren in each dif-frent place Will see the ba-by Je-sus' face Like

chil-dren see him lil-y white, With tress-es soft and fair. Some
chil-dren see him al-mond eyed, With skin of yel-low hue. Some
theirs, but bright with heav'n-ly grace, And filled with ho-ly light. O

chil-dren see him bronzed and brown, The Lord of heav'n to earth come down; Some
chil-dren see him dark as they, Sweet Mar-y's Son to whom we pray; Some
lay a-side each earth-ly thing, And with thy heart as of-fer-ing, Come

chil-dren see him bronzed and brown, With dark and heav-y hair.
chil-dren see him dark as they, And ah! they love him too!
wor-ship now the in-fant King. 'Tis love that's born to-night!

We'll Dress the House

Wihla Hutson · Alfred Burt

1. We'll dress the house with hol-ly bright And sprigs of mis-tle-
2. We'll dress the ta-ble dain-ti-ly, Our fin-est treas-ures
3. And ye who would the Christ child greet Your heart al-so a-

toe; We'll trim the Christ-mas tree to-night And
use, That all a-spar-kle it may be And
dorn, That it may be a dwell-ing meet For

set the lights a-glow; We'll wrap our gifts with
bright with love-ly hues; Then for the feast-ing
him who now is born. Let all un-love-ly

rib-bons gay And give them out on Christ-mas Day; By
we'll pre-pare A kitch-en full of won-drous fare, That
things give place To souls be-decked with heav'n-ly grace, That

ev-'ry-thing we do and say, Our glad-ness we will show.
each from all the dish-es rare, His fav-'rite one may choose.
ye may view his ho-ly face, With joy on Christ-mas morn.

All Saints'

Wihla Hutson wit...

Dad Burt

melva

In These United States

Christmas in Serbian, Russian-German, Vietnamese, and Creole Communities

LA VERN J. RIPPLEY

One of the great mysteries of world history is that the United States, alone among nations, has been able to imbibe the peoples of the globe with little indigestion. Like Christmas itself, this miracle deserves not only to be noted, but from time to time to be celebrated, for it signifies the larger Christmas ideal of unity. We shall consider here the Christmas customs of Americans from far-flung regions: the Serbs from Yugoslavia, the Creoles from France, the Germans from Russia, and the Vietnamese from Indochina.

Why consider these unrelated traditions together? For two basic reasons: To focus on America's unique assimilative capacity, and to portray the unifying power of Christ's birth. The United States at the federal level scarcely acknowledges the existence of immigrants. Actually, America simply has been here for those who wanted to join. The common denominator among the traditions lies in the nature of Christmas itself. One Christ was born for the many. The Christmas and New Year's customs practiced by four very different peoples illustrate more similarity than diversity. First the Serbs.

Serbia is one of six socialist republics (along with Croatia, Slovenia, Bosnia-Herzegovina, Montenegro, and Macedonia) that make up modern-day Yugoslavia. Sometimes referred to as Serbo-Croatian, the Serbian language is basically the same as that spoken by the Croats, except that Croats use the Latin alphabet while the Serbs employ the Cyrillic script. A more fundamental difference is that of religion: Croatians are Roman Catholic while Serbs are Orthodox. The Renaissance, the Reformation, and the Enlightenment had a strong influence on Croatia, but Serbia identified with Byzantium.

Beginning in the 12th century, Serbia enjoyed the benevolent leadership of Stephen Nemanya. His son Rastka founded the independent Serbian Orthodox Church. Later Serbia fell under the domination of the Ottoman Turks who ruled until modern times. Because the Turks often destroyed church buildings, Christian rituals were often sustained by village priests in family homes. So, too, the Christmas festivities focus around the hearth more than the altar.

The Orthodox Christmas, *Bozic,* follows the Eastern calendar, which coincides with January 7 on our Western calendar. *Materice* (Mother's Day) and *Ocevi* (Father's Day) are celebrated on the two Sundays preceding Christmas. These feasts call for gifts of cookies, fruit, clothing, and toys. Often the gifts are disguised in the parents' bedroom, perhaps under the covers or behind the bed, so that when the children sneak in early on those two mornings they are amply rewarded.

The Serbian Christmas itself calls for participation not just by the children but by the extended family. A few days before the feast folks in rural areas slaughter a pig, a ram, or an ewe for the holiday meal. Then the day before Christmas one of the menfolk heads for the woods to cut a young oak tree. About nightfall on Christmas Eve, a chosen member of the family fetches the Yule log or *Badnjak* cut from this oak, lights one sprig, and ignites the hearth with it. If there is no fireplace, the bearer thrusts the log into the stove exclaiming, *"Hristos se rodi!"* ("Christ is born!") Following an exchange of good wishes for health, prosperity, and happiness, another two logs are carried in and put on the hearth or in the stove. Then the head of the household bows down to kiss the ends protruding from the fire. Signing himself three times in the name of the Father, the Son, and the Holy Ghost, he utters the words, "As I have kissed this Yule log, may the cow have calves, the ewe lambs, the sow piglets, the hen chicks, and may every soul in my household have happiness and a productive year!"

The next ceremony is for children. Hoisting a large sack stuffed with straw over his shoulder, a young man of the household carries it outdoors followed by women and children who pluck at the sack. Imitating hens the women cry, *"Kvok, kvok, kvok,"* while the children hop gleefully behind cheeping, *"Piju, piju, piju,"* in the manner of young chicks. The entourage circles the house three times to honor the Trinity before returning inside. The straw is then scattered on the kitchen floor to symbolize that Christ was born in a stable, and the family sits down to a pre-Christmas repast. But first the family lights a tall candle, kindles a pot of incense, and prays together. In many villages the meal consists of braided bread for the females and bread in the shape of various livestock for male members. This meal, called the *Orasac,* concludes with a cake filled with apples and nuts and baked with sunflower seed oil because normal lard is prohibited during the fast. In most villages the straw remains on the floor all three days of Christmas and all meals are eaten upon it. Sometimes family members sleep on the straw, facing east to symbolize the direction from which Christ, the Light of the world, would come.

An old superstition in the Serbian countryside holds that an undesirable first caller on Christmas morning will bring disaster to the family during the coming year. In order to counteract this possibility, households carefully pick a male child to go outdoors shortly after sunrise, knock on the door for admittance, and in this way qualify as the first guest *(Polaznik).* Upon entering, this child calls out the same words uttered the previous eve-

Russian-German

ning, "Christ is born!" Sometimes the mother of the family tosses a small handful of grain on the boy as he enters to welcome him who symbolizes the Christ child. Next the youngster proceeds to the hearth or stove where the Yule log from the previous evening has turned to embers. With a fresh branch from the *Badnjak* he strikes the log to make sparks fly and chants, "As sparks fly from this fire, so may health, happiness, and goodwill burst forth from the people of our household." Any others in the home who wish to may repeat the gesture and blessing.

About noon the family reclines again on the straw to partake of the holiday fare. Although the food varies, bread is an absolute must and often is baked in an outdoor oven. A special Christmas loaf of bread (*Chesnica*) is baked containing a coin; whoever gets that loaf is considered very lucky. When extracted, this coin is glued to the ceiling with a sticky dough to protect the whole family during the following year. Sometimes mothers cleverly implant a coin in each little loaf so no child is disappointed. This ritual usually takes place at the beginning of the meal when all break bread together, sharing their loaves with the others in the family.

Meat and vegetables, highly seasoned with peppers, garlic, and salt, are often served as a stew. Another dish features a pastry filled with the ingredients of a stew, but shaped like a pie and cut in wedges. Stuffed peppers or cabbages are common fare, and rice often is served with highly seasoned chopped pork sausages. Roast suckling pig is a favorite at the Serbian-American Christmas dinner. Also popular are *Palacinke,* thin pancakes made from eggs, milk, and flour, which are fried in lard and served rolled up with prune jam inside. Another specialty is a white cheese loaf made from cow's milk, which is reminiscent of cottage cheese. Finally, there are small square cookies embossed with a waffle pattern, which are served only at Christmas. Adults conclude the meal with their favorite winter drink, Sumadijan tea.

In the United States many of these customs have been modified, although straw on the floor, the yule branch, and most food items persist. Early immigrants from Serbo-Croatia and Slovenia settled first in the New Orleans oyster region, but later they were attracted to the vineyards and fishing industry in California. When mass immigration began after 1890, an estimated one million moved to the industrial regions with the largest contingent of 170,000 settling in Pennsylvania, followed by Ohio, Illinois, Michigan, New York, Minnesota, California, and Wisconsin. The majority were Croatian, followed, in order, by Slovenian and Serbian.

The Germans who came from Russia shared with their East European counterparts a strong religious and folkloric tenacity which has preserved many ethnic customs.

The rich St. Nicholas tradition surrounding his feast day on December 6 as well as Christmas Day was easily transferred to Russia. The Germans found that St. Nicholas was no stranger to the steppes. Indeed, in the Czarist tradition he stood guard year around as the patron saint of Russia. So, in the German colonies he thrived, although bearing many versions of the same name depending on the dialect.

Called *Nickel* or *Klaus* for short, he usually conveyed a feeling of dread. Garbled remnants of *Pelznickel*, literally "the Nicholas in fur," strike the ear as *Belzenickel, Bullerklas,* and *Pelzmarte.* Sometimes clothed in goatskin, he took on the adulterated names of *Belzebock* and even *Beelzebub,* clearly identifying Nicholas not just with fear but with Satan himself.

On the other hand, the *Christkindlein* (sometimes called *Christkindel*) of Russian-German tradition was a figure bringing light and joy. In the settlement days of the Dakotas, Nebraska, and Kansas, the *Christkindlein* brought the gifts to Russian-German homes. Sometimes families would arrange for an appearance of *Christkindel* halfway through the Advent season for just a fleeting moment. She would knock on a window until recognized, then throw in a handful of candy and disappear into the night. Mothers used the occasion to admonish their children to build and decorate cardboard baskets to be set out for *Christkindel* on Christmas Eve. Formerly, Russian-German custom mandated that *Christkindel* arrive on a donkey. In the German dialects of the Dakotas and Kansas are preserved doggerel about "setting out refreshments for the passenger and a bundle of hay for the beast of burden."

Christmas for children of a Russian-German family was often a mixture of great joy and fear—fear of the *Pelznickel,* and joy over the *Christkindel's* visit. On Christmas Eve, the *Christkindel,* usually a woman dressed in a long, flowing white gown and wearing a gold crown or long streamers of colored ribbon, would knock on the door. In some communities she wore on her head the circlet of candles associated with the Lucia figure of Swedish tradition. The *Pelznickel* would accompany her. A strong, burly young lad, the *Pelznickel* always wore a sheepskin (preferably black) with the wool turned out on his head, a heavy ceremonial fur hat. Often he displayed horns from the sides of his head, a heavy chain around his neck, and a stick or bundle of switches in his left hand.

In omniscience, the *Christkindlein* always knew every youngster's good deeds and bad deeds; each child had to answer for the past year and promise excellent behavior in the coming year. For the bad child there was at least a light dusting of the backsides, which elicited the promise not to provoke any complaints the next year. For the good child there were words of praise and encouragement. Next, the *Christkindlein* passed out apples, nuts, cookies, and sweets before disappearing into the darkness of the night with *Pelznickel* clanging a step or two behind.

Parents, catechism teachers, and parish pastors were careful to keep the *Christkindlein* and the *Pelznickel* alive throughout the year. The two Christmas figures functioned as a carrot stick, modifying children's behavior toward hard work, orderliness, learning, and the like. Always Christmas was in the offing when it came to either rewards or punishment (the latter always more in anticipation than in reality). Russian-German adults, like the Serbs, did not exchange gifts at Christmas. This was strictly a children's event.

Although deeply rooted in German tradition, the *Christbaum* or Christmas tree was not one of the practices that the Germans took with them to the plains of South Russia. Rather, an older Christmas tradition prevailed, especially along the Volga, one which the German settlers brought from Russia to western Kansas. Instead of a pine or fir tree, cherry or lilac branches were cut three weeks before Christmas and submerged in water, so that the buds burst into bloom about Christmas Eve. Similarly, these rural people also developed the tradition of planting seeds of wheat or barley in a wooden box about three weeks prior to Christmas, so there would be plenty of greenery in the house at Christmastime. These branches and boxes were decorated with nuts, ornaments, and ribbons. The wheat box always served as a centerpiece on the Christmas dinner table.

million Indochinese, the vast majority of whom were Vietnamese, had settled in the United States.

Since the dominant religion of Vietnam is Buddhism, the celebration of Christmas is limited to the Christian communities, which are largest in the big cities. And since the lunar calendar rather than the Gregorian system used in the West determines the dates of festivities, Christmas falls near the end of January or the beginning of February rather than on December 25. The *Tet* or New Year's celebration is the major national event rather than the commemoration of the birth of Christ. Nevertheless, the French presence in Vietnam beginning in the 1860s brought Christianity to the area. Christmas found a place in the hearts and minds not only of the 20 percent who became Catholic but even of non-Christian Vietnamese.

Serbian

The Indochinese presence in the United States, like the Yugoslavian and Russian-German, is a composite of formerly separate ethnic groups who have maintained their identities in the United States. Among the immigrants are Vietnamese, Chinese, Hmong, Lao, and Cambodians. While all of their cultures have common features, the groups differ vastly in historic origins, religious beliefs, occupations, life-styles, as well as language. For our purposes we shall consider only the Vietnamese whose presence in the United States grew rapidly following the cessation of American involvement in their homeland in 1975. By the early 1980s at least one-half

In Vietnam there is no commemoration of Advent. Instead the Christmas season gets underway about two weeks before the holiday when shoppers throng into the streets to purchase toys and gifts to exchange with relatives and friends. Presents are rarely exchanged on Christmas Eve; rather, they are delivered directly to the homes of recipients, generally before Christmas. Most homes are decorated with artificial trees unless real pines are available. Following the European tradition, Christmas trees are lighted by candles rather than electric lights. A typical decoration in every home is the Christmas cake-log. This is often the gift of a good friend or relative. The cake can be either chocolate or white and is usually coated with a butter creme frosting and sprinkled with chocolate shavings.

Because South Vietnam and the capital city of Saigon, in particular, lie in a semitropical region, Christmas is not a snowy, wintry scene. With temperatures in the 80s on Christmas Eve, people flock into the streets in order to exchange good wishes with acquaintances and strangers alike. At midnight, mass is celebrated in churches that are jammed to capacity. The cathedral, the square, and the streets fill up early on Christmas Eve, so that parishioners extend a mile from the main altar, hearing, if not exactly attending, the service. There are no additional masses on Christmas Day. Unique circumstances dictate why Christmas Eve in Saigon became so special. For decades the city had curfew laws, which took effect

mon in Vietnamese churches and homes, but not in shops and on street corners as in the United States. Santa Claus, too, has been imported and makes his rounds rewarding children who have been well-behaved. The traditional letter to Santa, however, is not mailed to a local newspaper but is burned, perhaps after showing it to one's parents. On Christmas Eve, Vietnamese children hang socks or leave their shoes near the bed for Santa to fill with candy. Then, on Christmas Day the Vietnamese eat a traditional meal of roast chicken served with rice and plenty of egg rolls, and capped with a bounteous piece of the aforementioned Yule cake-log.

New Year's or *Tet* in the Vietnamese tradition is a time of thanksgiving for life and family. The three days of *Tet* are set aside to remember one's family—the entire extended family, including ancestors and friends who have

Vietnamese

at either 10:00 or 11:00 P.M. On Christmas Eve, however, the curfew was lifted, making the streets available for festivities throughout the night. Christmas celebrations often lasted beyond the conclusion of mass to the wee hours of the morning.

To Americans of European heritage, Christmas has always been first and foremost a family affair. Not so for the Vietnamese. To them, Christmas involves the whole community; it is a social event celebrated by the entire city regardless of religious affiliation. The Vietnamese sing Christmas carols in the Western tradition, with lyrics in Vietnamese. The Christmas crèche is com-

passed away. To the Vietnamese, the new year suggests new life, like the first day of spring. In celebration of life and community, people visit each other's homes to wish them the best for the coming year. The eldest of the family are greeted first, then other relatives on down the ranks of the extended line. At each household, the host offers a toast and customarily gives a few coins to the children who have come. In anticipation of this custom, adults carry up to 100 red envelopes containing a few coins in their pockets to distribute to youngsters who wish them a happy new year.

Characteristic of most oriental New Year's Eve celebrations is the shooting of firecrackers, allegedly to frighten away evil spirits and, of course, to welcome in the new year.

In the Vietnamese tradition, what happens on New Year's Day will determine how the whole year will go. Like the Serbs, wise families make provisions for a prominent family member to drop by early. If the visitor is himself happy, handsome, and, if possible, wealthy, that will have significance for the entire household throughout the year. Another tradition advises families not to bother sweeping the house during *Tet*, for then they will be brushing off wealth, good fortune, and happiness. At this time, too, it's a bad omen to lose one's temper or to swear, for this will surely bring evil upon the family.

Since the dragon and the angel are the two most powerful figures in the Vietnamese story of creation, these characters also appear in the New Year's ceremony. They personify the two ever-present natural forces that work upon the Vietnamese life and mind—the sea and the mountains. The dragon derives from the sea, the angel from the mountains. Together they begot all the people of that long, slender nation. In the New Year's ceremony, this peculiar geographic situation is dramatized.

It's a long leap from Vietnam to the Creoles of Louisiana, but the French have influenced the customs of both places. The word *creole* may be confusing because it is used occasionally in its original meaning for a slave brought up in the owner's household. More often it denotes Europeans born in the Caribbean of foreign-born colonists. In Louisiana, however, the word came into use after the Louisiana Purchase in 1803 when local inhabitants of French ancestry sought to distinguish themselves from the Anglo-Americans who began moving into the new territory. Louisiana Creoles can be of either white French background or of black ancestry. We focus here on the Creoles of French ethnicity, who are primarily at home in New Orleans.

Fundamentally a religious festival, the Creole Christmas has a definitely French accent. Creoles traditionally had large families, and their gatherings at this time of the year alternated between hearth and altar without the slightest Puritanical restraint. During the early hours of Christmas Eve, extended families assemble at the hearth. By 10:00 P.M., the first church bells peal, summoning all to midnight mass. Not even a confirmed agnostic Creole would dare to miss mass and so incur the social displeasure. Sitting in church awaiting the magic hour of 12:00 affords the chance to visit with friends. But with the first clang of midnight all whispering dies out as the organ heralds the solemn event.

After mass comes the *reveillon* or Christmas breakfast, featuring eggs, sweetbreads, raisin cake, and the specialties of each particular family. Topping it all off is a rum cake capped with plenty of whipped cream and strong black coffee. Sleep comes, though fitfully, for in a few hours children will be up to learn whether Papa Noël has paid a visit.

In the Creole tradition, as with the Serbs, Russian-Germans, and Vietnamese, children do not receive major gifts from relatives and neighbors at Christmastime. That is reserved for the New Year's festival. In a locked room Papa Noël has prearranged candy and small toys in stockings or, perhaps, dangled them from a small Christmas tree, which has been festooned with ribbons. This touch of a Germanic tradition was added in later years. The French custom originally called for a sizable crèche rather than an evergreen tree. As with the Germans from Russia, branches cut from a fruit tree and placed in water proved sufficient to remind the family of the new birth on Christmas Day.

In today's Creole home Papa Noël might make an appearance, looking not unlike his American cousin all dressed in red and white. He jovially admonishes older children and carefully rewards younger believers. This visit takes on deeper meaning when children are taken to mass where they view the life-sized crèche in one of the churches in the French Quarter. From the altar they return again to the hearth and, especially, to the kitchen for a superb banquet with family members.

New Year's Eve is even more festive and certainly more active with singing and dancing than is Christmas. Like the Vietnamese, the Creoles believe that as goes New Year's Day, so goes the whole year. Thus it is important to meet successful and happy persons early in the day. Special verses help children wish their parents, grandparents, uncles, and aunts just the right kind of new year so that they in turn will aid the younger generation during the year. It is doubly important for children to repeat the correct formula because this is the day they receive major holiday gifts—toys, dolls, a wagon, an embroidered dress, or tin soldiers in Napoleonic uniforms. As in the Vietnamese tradition, the young are obligated to pay a visit to those higher in age or authority. Calls are made to favorite aunts, grandparents, and older married brothers and sisters if they are not at home for the family gathering. In turn, it is important that children stay home themselves for part of the day in order to receive well-wishers and gifts.

Later in the afternoon the family gathers for a traditional meal, often consisting of gumbo made with shrimp and crabmeat or chicken plus a dozen other ingredients. There are plenty of pralines, cakes, and coffee, often glorified with spirits, cinnamon, or the shreds of orange and lemon peels. If the coffee is strong enough to be set afire, it is called *cafe diabolique*, which captures the attention of the household. The lights are lowered so that the tongues of fire will cast dancing shadows on the walls. While many of the customs and traditions of the Creoles today are disappearing, the latter has been adopted by many residents and restaurateurs of New Orleans.

Truly, proving the origin of these holiday practices is not the appropriate quest. What is of consequence is that the Christmas spirit has traveled well. It links the Orthodox Serbian village with the German-Russian community on the Great Plains; it unites Vietnamese families from Saigon with the Creoles of New Orleans. At Christmas, the overarching fact of Christ's birth brings us all together. Whatever our culture, we unite at the manger of the Christ child right here in these United States.

Creole

Nativity

John Singleton Copley, 1738-1815

PHILLIP GUGEL

Copley's *Nativity* captures the shepherds' awe and excitement over the Christ child. Though hundreds of European artists painted this subject, a particularly popular one during the Counter-Reformation era, only a very few American artists have left us pictures of it. While Copley's composition draws on the influences of Italian Renaissance and Baroque painting, it includes features peculiar to this American artist as well.

Susannah Farnum, Copley's wife and source of inspiration, served as his model for Mary. Instead of showing her kneeling or sitting, Mary's usual pose since the Gothic period, he painted a reclining virgin as in earlier Byzantine versions. Here she supports herself on her

right arm, with her hand on her forehead. Preoccupied with her infant son, she seems oblivious of their visitors. Her elongated body in its exotic white costume of uncertain origin dominates the foreground and becomes Copley's ideal image of Mary and motherhood. These white garments deviate from the traditional blue and red ones of many other pictures.

One of his daughters (also named Susannah), an infant when he painted the *Nativity* in 1776, found her way into the picture as Copley's model for the Christ child. Like Mary's, Jesus' delicate white complexion contrasts with the ruddy faces of Joseph and the shepherds. Fast asleep, he seems well protected beneath his mother's gaze. The attentive dog near them symbolizes faithfulness and watchfulness in traditional Christian iconography. Copley's broad triangular arrangement of these figures fills most of the foreground.

The whiteness of Mary's clothing and the Christ child's bedding contrasts with the rug's warm colors. Copley's delight in color and the appearance of varied materials is evident in the rug's colors, its detailed fringe, stripes, and texture, as well as in the stalks of grain protruding from the straw pile on which it rests. This rug becomes our visual entry point into the picture from the bottom, a device commonly used by Renaissance and Baroque painters. In artistic parlance such an entry point into the composition is known by its French term, *repoussoir*.

The ruddy faces, finely delineated curly hair, and brightly colored clothing of Joseph and the shepherds also show Copley's enjoyment in painting color and texture. He treated all surfaces equally. Their colored clothing also sets off the pale figures of mother and child, swathed in white.

Joseph's green-clad, husky figure suggests Michelangelo's influence; while his robust, smiling, and youthful face contrasts with Mary's delicate and detached features. Engaged in animated conversation with the shepherds, he seems more involved in their visit, unlike those examples where he is shown as an elderly, saintly man, silently keeping watch.

Although the older, brown-clad shepherd at the upper left, whose features suggest a facial type associated with St. Peter, seems rather solemn, his three brawny, handsome companions are more demonstrative. As a *repoussoir* figure on the left side, the blue-clad shepherd points out the Christ child to someone unseen, while the yellow-clad companion in front of him holds up his hands in astonishment. Copley's gesturing shepherds charge his composition with excitement in contrast to Mary's gesture of calm detachment. Figural gestures were another device fully exploited by Renaissance and Baroque painters.

Above Joseph and the shepherds diagonal rays of light from an unseen source repeat their diagonal arrangement and spatial recession, while the long diagonal begun by Mary at the lower right and continued by Joseph and three of the shepherds into the upper left, unifies their figures and draws us into the composition.

To the right, Copley's triangular arrangement of the cattle, donkey, and unidentified man balances his triangular arrangement of Joseph and the shepherds and completes the backdrop for the Christ child and Mary. His placement of one figure behind another creates a sense of spatial recession. On this edge of the picture the man and donkey in its stall function as entry points into the composition. They also balance the blue-clad shepherd, just as the huge cattle in their carefully painted russet and white coats balance Joseph and the two shepherds next to him. The Christ child and the upper half of Mary are the apex of a triangle formed by diagonals coming toward us from the top of the canvas. All of these linear devices help balance and unify the figures.

Beyond the man and cattle, an imaginary moonlit landscape, another Baroque influence, completes Copley's composition, although it makes an odd contrast with the light rays on the left. His inclusion of a lake or river in the landscape is unusual, although a body of water was common in earlier nativity scenes, particularly those by the Flemish masters.

Copley finished the *Nativity* in December 1776, and exhibited it at the Royal Academy in London the following year. Then the canvas disappeared until 1864, when it was placed on sale, only to disappear again until it was mistakenly auctioned off as one of Benjamin West's paintings in 1971. When the picture was correctly identified as Copley's, the Museum of Fine Arts, Boston, purchased it in December 1972, to add to its large collection of his works. In 1976, the *Nativity* received national circulation as a reproduction on a Christmas postage stamp during the Bicentennial year, a fitting tribute to America's most famous colonial painter.

Despite his lack of formal artistic training, Copley became a successful portrait painter by 1765. But like other artists following him, he was frustrated by his isolation from European art and by the lack of interest, except for portraits, which Americans showed in the visual arts. He dreamed of becoming a history painter, since at that time painting biblical, historical, and mythological subjects was the most prestigious career an artist could have. In the midst of worsening relations between England and the 13 colonies, he left Boston in 1774 on a study tour of European art. In 1775 his wife and children joined him in London, where they settled. Copley never returned to America, but strived to prove himself a history painter abroad.

Although he may not have resolved all of the technical aspects of the *Nativity's* composition perfectly, this important transitional picture in Copley's career left us a fresh interpretation of an overly popular subject—which is all the more valuable since so few American artists after Copley have painted it. As we celebrate the incarnation, Copley's *Nativity* reminds us of the shepherds' awe and excitement, once their fears had vanished, at Christ's coming to his people. This gift of wonder is ours as well, as we delight in Copley's proclamation that "God is with us."

The Warmth of a Quilt

SALLY GRAUER

Christmas dreams are happier under a Christmas quilt, I like to think. When I was a child my mother made me a quilt I got to use only during the Christmas season. Until the middle of December it was stored on a special shelf with sachet tucked inside. The ceremony of taking the quilt down from the shelf and putting it on my bed was an event I looked forward to with great anticipation. —Bonnie Leman

This splendid Album Quilt was appliquéd for a Christmas bride, c. 1950.

Christmas is a quilter's delight. What better time of year to fill the house with the warmth of homemade things, to create family traditions to enjoy and to pass on to future generations.

Patchwork quilting is pure Americana. This wonderful art form was developed by our ancestors out of need, the need for warmth in the New World.

When the Pilgrims boarded the *Mayflower* for their great adventure, family quilts were packed safely away in the baggage. Little did they know just what a vital role their quilts would play.

The ship offered no conveniences to the passengers and certainly no comforts. They had to provide all their own necessities, including food and bedding. Quilts were used on the shelf beds aboard ship; some were hung up as a sort of curtain to afford a little privacy during the long voyage.

By the time the Pilgrims reached the New World, the quilts as well as their clothing were badly worn. Patching worn-out quilts had never been necessary before. Old quilts had simply been discarded or used as rags by English homemakers. But in the colonies cloth was scarce and new clothing was an absolute necessity.

So, Pilgrim women did clouting or, as we know it today, patching. They tried to make their blankets and quilts last until new cloth arrived from England. They patched and patched until the cloth would no longer take the thread.

Meanwhile, to safeguard its own economy, England restricted the delivery of goods to the colonies. The colonies could receive only English goods on English ships, and they could produce only those things needed by England. The manufacture of cloth was particularly prohibited. Flax seed, sheep, and the tools necessary to make cloth were considered contraband; smugglers faced harsh jail terms if they were caught helping the colonists. If they were caught a second time, smugglers often lost a hand or even their lives.

Even so, more people slipped through the patrols than were caught. By 1640, the manufacture of cloth in the northern colonies was well under way. Other colonies soon followed. Even though the cloth industry flourished, acquiring cloth was still a long process. It took a full year to grow a crop of flax and still more time to prepare the flax for the spinning wheel and to make cloth. During the waiting period, women continued to patch.

Then, a Pilgrim woman pieced together the scraps from her cutting table after making new garments for her family and created a new quilt top. The quilt was filled with corn husks or grasses; instead of fine quilting stitches, string tied in knots at intervals held the quilt layers together. That was the first American quilt.

Such quilts were a far cry from the beautiful woven blankets and finely quilted coverlets the women were accustomed to in England. But the quilts were warm, and that was all that mattered. Quilts covered the beds and also the doors and windows to keep out the cold winds.

As life became a little easier for the women, they found time to blend beauty with necessity. They took great pride in making their scrap quilts not only warm, but also pleasing to the eye. It was a challenge to use every snip of precious cloth and to work out intricate geo-

(top) The Star of Bethlehem shines from this pieced quilt, c. 1930.
(bottom) Bethlehem in colorful appliqué adorns this contemporary quilt.

metric designs and brilliant color combinations. Some of the early quilts had thousands of pieces in them. Yet, the women who worked out the intricate designs within each block of the quilt had no knowledge of mathematics at all.

What began as a necessity quickly became a means of artistic expression for the women. Besides the need for protection against harsh New England winters, they needed a touch of beauty in their lives. Even in the most crude log cabin, the mistress of the house wanted her home to be as attractive as possible. Since the bed was often the focal point in the small structure, she tried to make the quilt covering it beautiful. The fact that each scrap was a reminder of loved ones made the quilts even more special. Scraps from grandmother's wedding dress were lovingly pointed out to the grandchildren.

Along with the need for beauty in their spartan lives, women also longed for the companionship of other women. There was very little time for socializing. Work at home and on the farm came first. Though neighbors gathered for barn raisings and cornhuskings, those events were hard work and involved the whole family. Only the quilting bee was a special event just for women.

Quilting bees were usually held in the spring. After a long winter with only husbands and children for company, it was a treat to dress up a bit and spend the day with friends. A bee provided a time for conversation and even a little competition. It was a luxury to spend the day doing something one enjoyed.

For many years the bee was the most popular form of hospitality among women. There was even a "pecking order" of sorts. The best quilters were invited first, then the friends of the hostess. Friends who were not the best quilters were asked to cook, which they usually did willingly.

Besides patchwork piecing, another quilting skill became popular during Revolutionary War times—appliqué. Appliqué comes from the French word meaning to "lay on" and dates back at least 3000 years. During the Crusades it was done to decorate the clothing of knights. The technique involves fabric designs which are permanently applied to a background fabric.

American appliqué was created out of necessity, just as patchwork was. In 1701 the Act of Parliament forbade the import of Indian painted calico fabrics. Wide beds were in vogue at that time and women never had enough of the beautiful calicoes to cover them. So they cut out the fruit and flower designs and appliquéd them on unbleached fabric, which was more readily available.

The appliqué quilt was most popular in the South. Fewer quilts were needed because of the warm climate, so the women had more time for the fancier handwork. And, of course, they had servants to help.

By 1850, the appliqué technique was the design of choice for a woman's masterpiece quilt. Elaborate floral appliqué became such a status symbol that often, after a woman had labored over her quilt, she felt it was too special for anything more than display. Today many of those quilts can be found in museums.

One of the best known and most beautiful appliqué patterns is the Rose of Sharon. Eighteenth century quilters went to the Bible for its name. From the Song of Solomon came these words:

> I am the rose of Sharon,
>   And the lily of the valleys.
> As the lily among thorns,
>   so is my love among the daughters;
> As the apple tree among the trees of the wood,
>   so is my beloved among the sons.

There are many variations of the Rose of Sharon pattern, with its rose flower, leaves, buds, and stems. It was used most often in the bride's quilt, not only because of

(top) The stars come out at night with this Christmas Star Sampler, a pieced quilt. (bottom) Dreams come true on Alex's Christmas Quilt of appliquéd reindeer and Christmas trees.

its beauty but also because of the love story told in the age-old poem.

Along with patchwork and appliqué, there is yet another style of quilting, one that takes a great deal of expertise. All-white or white-on-white quilts are made from two sheets of white cloth with a filler in between. The entire surface is elaborately hand quilted with white thread. With no color or fabric pattern to distract the

50

A 1930s Poinsettia pattern is revived on this bold appliqué quilt.

eye, fine even stitches are a must. The result is an amazingly subtle quilted design.

The invention of the sewing machine changed almost all hand sewing. Many women chose to use their time differently, and the elegant all-white quilt almost disappeared. Those still being made are usually done only by expert quilters.

The naming of quilt patterns is an interesting custom, as old as quilting itself. Some have been named for popular sayings, such as "The Pure Symbol of Right Doctrine" from the Quakers, as well as for tools and things around the house. Political figures as well as their parties were favorites too. Legend has it that a certain quiet but strong woman never let her Whig husband know that he slept under a Democrat Rose quilt each night. In addition, there were Lincoln's Platform, Clay's Choice, Washington's Quilt, and Jackson's Star.

The most popular quilt pattern names were usually religious or floral. Some old favorites include Star of Bethlehem, Jacob's Ladder, Rose of Sharon, King David's Crown, Crown of Thorns, and Joseph's Coat.

Floral favorites always included Grandmother's Flower Garden and Sunflower. Sunflower patterns were very popular during the nineteenth century. They were usually done in natural sunflower colors of brown and yellow. Other favorites were the tulip patterns and lily designs, both of which were bright and colorful.

Tree patterns have been around since colonial times. The Pine Tree meant loyalty and steadfastness and was often used by New England quilters. Other tree designs were Tree of Life, Tree of Temptation, Tree of Paradise, and Little Beech Tree.

Some quilt patterns were named especially for holidays. The Christmas Rose was created in the 1840s. Usually done in reds and greens are also the Christmas Star and Christmas Tree.

One of the oldest and best-loved quilting patterns is the Log Cabin with its many variations. The blocks are created by geometric arrangement of strips of fabric. The strips on the four sides of the block represent the logs and the small center square symbolizes the fireplace, the heart of the home. The most common Log Cabin was made of dark woolen strips with a bright red centerpiece as the only spot of color. Some were made with yellow centers, representing the firelight. Those quilts were an integral part of most every colonial home.

One reason the Log Cabin has maintained its popularity over the years is its many variations. Along with the humble woolen version of the Log Cabin, wonderfully elegant and fanciful ones were made of satin, silk, and velvet pieces. In a private collection, there is an all-white satin Log Cabin quilt dating back to the later 1800s. It was presumably made from scraps of a wedding gown.

The Victorian Crazy Quilt was a basically unusable quilt made of silks and velvets and ribbons and even bits of lace. The pieces were cut in odd shapes and held together with decorative embroidery stitches. It had no batting (filling) as it was impossible to quilt through the various fabrics. These elegant quilts often wound up as throws on a horsehair sofa in the parlor or, perhaps, draped over a piano.

The Crazy Quilt survived well into the 1920s, as did the quilting bee. Down through the years the bee became more of a church quilting event, but still an important occasion for women. It is said that Susan B. Anthony made her first speech advocating the vote for women at a church quilting bee.

Certain groups of women have made special contributions as quiltmakers. The Pennsylvania Dutch are probably the most proficient and original of American quiltmakers. Their designs are wonderfully bold, done in strong, bright colors. Patterns with curved seams are usually found in the designs, making them by far the most difficult to piece.

Pennsylvania Dutch women were not taught to read or write, so quilting became of great importance to them. It provided a lasting record of themselves.

Another group of superb quilters is the Amish. The Amish are deeply puritanical people. Their religion forbids any outward decoration just for decoration's sake. Therefore, Amish quilts are traditionally done in solid color fabrics as opposed to print fabrics. The use of vivid colors in unlikely combinations is just part of what makes Amish quilts unique. Today the starkly beautiful quilts of the Amish are very much in demand by collectors.

Quilts also have been a part of the Mormon heritage for many generations. When persecution drove them across the country to Utah, they made quilts as did all pioneers. The difference was the Mormons never stopped quilting.

The Relief Society is the Mormon Church women's organization. For many years, quilting has been an integral part of its monthly meetings. The church encourages quilting as an art form, as well as a homemaking skill. Speed is not of great importance. Creativity and fine stitches are.

The Relief Society General Office in downtown Salt Lake City has a permanent quilt display which is open to tourists as well as to Relief Society members. The display quilts are changed every six months, giving many women an opportunity to show their work and to exchange ideas on color and design with others.

Many customs surrounded the art of quilting. One was the Baker's Dozen. A young girl was expected to have made 12 quilts for her dowry chest by the time she was ready to marry. These quilts were made for everyday use. The girl pieced them herself, beginning when she was little. When she became definitely engaged, the thirteenth quilt, which was the bride's quilt, was done. Traditionally, the bride's quilt was an elaborate design of hearts and flowers. It was considered bad luck for the bride to sew her own wedding quilt. Friends gathered together and did the quilting as a gift of love.

The art of quiltmaking also is not without superstition. One superstitious idea supposedly came back from the Orient on the China Clippers. The belief was that only God could create something absolutely perfect. For a mere mortal to create something without flaw was tempting the Devil and misfortune was sure to follow. Most quilters in the early 1800s did not wish to tempt fate, so their quilts were made with one blue leaf or one green flower. Better to be safe than sorry.

Another superstition involved the heart shape. Hearts were reserved for bride's quilts only and were considered unlucky for anyone else.

Quilts for boys were not without superstition either. There was a pattern called Wandering Foot, and no mother would ever make a quilt with that pattern for her son. Wandering foot meant the same as wanderlust, and the evil surrounding the design was so strong that any male who slept under it would soon leave home.

Since it was a pretty pattern, there had to be a way to use it. There was. A woman simply renamed the design Turkey Tracks, and the evil influence vanished.

Symbols also play an important role in quilting. The pineapple has long been the symbol of hospitality—not only in quilting. Much of post-colonial woodcarving involved the pineapple, as evidenced by the pineapple atop four-poster beds.

In the early 1800s, the dove symbolized femininity and happy marriage. In those days, a group of young women getting together was called a "doves party."

The swastika was the symbol of fertility and of good fortune for thousands of years. It was a favorite symbol of early quiltmakers. Since it took on such a sinister meaning during World War II, the pattern is seldom used anymore.

Flowers used on a quilt had the same meaning as the real flowers. The daisy meant innocence and the lily stood for purity. And, of course, the red rose symbolized true love.

Even the displaying of quilts was governed by tradition in the old days. A woman could show only the quilts of which she had done every stitch herself. Those quilts were stacked one on top of the other on the guest bed in the house. When a guest prepared for bed, the quilts were removed and folded one at a time, allowing for each to be admired. Even Martha Washington displayed her quilts in that manner. It is said that she kept 15 to 20 quilts on the guest bed.

Today the Amish still practice that tradition. Every Old Order Amish family opens its home for church services at least once a year. At that time, the family is

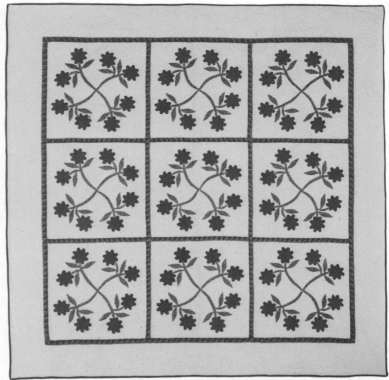

Piecework and appliqué appear on this festive Christmas Garland quilt.

allowed to display its fine quilts, thus encouraging the continued skill of quilt making.

The tradition of American quilting managed to survive down through the years, even when it was no longer a necessity. New quilts were created for special occasions, such as weddings and births and farewell presents. Many an outgoing minister was given a lovely friendship quilt by the women of the church.

In some areas the art of quilting was equated with poverty, and women no longer publicly admitted to their talents. Public interest in the old art of quilting waned.

There were some attempts to revive quilting. During the Great Depression the Parks Departments had quilting projects for women in addition to the tasks for men. But major interest in the old art declined.

The new quilting movement which began in the late sixties was somewhat different from times past. Women were interested in producing quality workmanship, but they were also interested in being innovative and creating new designs, not out of necessity but as an expression of art and creativity.

Quilt clubs sprang up all across the country, along with shops stocking all sorts of quilting supplies and offering classes for beginners to experts. There were juried shows and new magazines devoted to quilting.

Along with quilts, women began making wall hangings, articles of clothing, and all manner of things to decorate the home with a touch of Americana. Best of all were the holidays.

If you ask who comes to mind when thinking of Christmas, the answer is likely to be grandmother. Grandmother's house means turkey and stuffing and pumpkin pies. It also means a tree trimmed with old and wonderful ornaments and strung with popcorn and cranberries. And it means presents, and maybe a special quilt.

A sampler is a quilt in which every block is different. One loving grandmother made a Christmas sampler for her young grandchild. It had a house block done from a picture of the child's house next to a teddy bear block.

(top) Appliquéd angels in pigtails sing a lullaby on Katya's Angels Quilt. (bottom) Bright red flowers atop green plants bloom for the holidays on this Appliqué Quilt, c. 1870.

Christmas is the time to display those special treasures from the past, those handed down from generation to generation. A quilted table runner is a perfect backdrop for the ruby red glassware you might have inherited. And that antique cradle is a child's favorite with its tiny pieced patchwork quilt covering a china doll.

Wall hangings also herald the Christmas season. A madonna and child quilt design that resembles stained glass recalls the true meaning of Christmas.

Stained glass is a relatively new quilting technique. In place of the lead came that holds the pieces of glass together, the quilter uses bias strips of black fabric. Solid color fabrics are used to represent the glass pieces.

Many churches now have permanent collections of quilted banners for the celebration of Christmas, Easter, and other religious occasions. These banners allow the women who make them to express their own creativity as well as their faith.

Quilters usually begin quilting the day after Christmas and stop the following Christmas Eve. Besides Christmas tree ornaments, wreaths, tree skirts, and stockings to quilt, there are many gift items. Of course, a quilt makes a very special gift, but so does a patchwork vest or a cute stuffed animal.

A lovely gift might be a quilted wall hanging of the home of a friend or loved one, created in bright calico prints from a snapshot. A set of four placemats quilted in holiday colors also makes a thoughtful gift.

Handmade gifts are always appreciated. They are gifts of love that offer a little bit of oneself through the time and effort spent.

Every handmade gift is really a holiday heirloom, as handmade decorations continue to bring pleasure year after year when they are taken out of storage. They soon become part of the family Christmas tradition. After all, who can resist a batch of charming stuffed tree ornaments or a tree skirt appliqued with bright green sprigs of holly?

American patchwork quilting has come a long way since its humble beginning in colonial days. Quilting has met the physical needs by giving warmth through long, cold winters. Quilting also has answered the needs of women down through the years, both social needs and the need for creative expression.

Its popularity has waned from time to time, but the best part about the American tradition of quilting is that it never died. It has always played some part in the growth and development of this country.

The cycle continues. There are collectors who purchase old quilts for their beauty and monetary value. Family members cherish old quilts handed down from one generation to another. And, best of all, quilters are busy today creating the heirlooms of tomorrow.

The warmth of a Christmas quilt glows in the homes of many as family heirlooms are brought out and spread over the beds during the Christmas season. Memories of earlier Christmases when the one who made the quilt was present, of childhood anticipation, of family gatherings are all unbundled with the Christmas quilt. And, how can one separate those feelings of nostalgia from the childhood memories of cuddling, snug and warm, under grandmother's Christmas quilt. There is nothing so warm as a Christmas quilt.

There was a nativity scene block and one created from a first grade drawing the child had done. There was a Christmas stocking block and several toy blocks. Each block evoked memories of Christmases past.

Christmas patchwork can brighten up the entire house. A puffy red and green wreath can grace the front door or the space above the mantle. Poinsettias, an old pattern from the thirties, makes perfect throw pillows for an antique rocking chair.

A Frontier Christmas

BOB ARTLEY

The air had been unseasonably warm that morning when Paul hitched up the team and started out for Worthington, Minnesota. The fragrance of the wet sod was reminiscent of a spring day. However, there were no sounds of spring. The prairie-dwelling birds, such as meadowlarks, redwings, and killdeer, had long ago flown to a safer climate. The only sounds that broke the muffled silence enveloping this vast, trackless expanse had been the distant voices of some crows in the bare branches of the willows and cottonwoods along the creek. The only other sounds had been those made by the horses, Jim and Queen, and the wagon as they traveled through the tall ripened grasses.

The trail, being seldom used, was overgrown with tall grass and other prairie plants and was barely visible to the untrained eye. But Paul had a good sense of direction and could read the terrain well. He often liked to think of himself as a sailor guiding his small craft across an open sea. He had to navigate by the subtle landmarks of an occasional tree or rock, hummocks or shallow ravines, and steered clear of the creeks with their small tributaries and sink holes.

An important landmark, as far as their home was concerned, were two tall cottonwood trees that stood just a few feet apart on the northern boundary of their claim. The family had early decided those trees would be the gateway to their farm. Fourteen-year-old Tom thought they looked like sentinels at guard, so "the Sentinels" they

became. Paul felt at home in his adopted prairie place and confident as a traveler.

After Paul had been on the trail for about two hours, he noticed the overcast sky had become dark and threatening. A fine mist began to fall. It was only then that he was glad he had thought to bring the canvas, which was folded in a corner of the wagon box along with his great driving coat and wool-lined horsehide robe. The coat and robe had been Nora's idea.

Before long the mist turned to rain; and then, as the temperature dropped sharply, the wind began to blow and the rain turned to snow. By the time he arrived in Worthington, the snow was getting thicker by the moment. It was wet and heavy and stuck to everything.

Several teams, hitched to wagons or other rigs, were tied to the hitching rail in front of the depot. Paul had to search for a space to tie his own. The train had arrived only moments before so there was much activity. Travelers and those who had come to meet them created a larger crowd than normal for such a new outpost of civilization. Paul hadn't seen so many people gathered together for some time. The air was full not only of wind-driven snow but of the chatter and laughter of the crowd. The hissing engine, resting now after its long trip, provided a background accompaniment for the happy babble.

Not seeing his sister in the crowd on the station platform, Paul entered the depot. A noisy crowd was milling about inside too. Some were carrying colorful packages

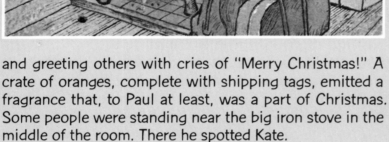

and greeting others with cries of "Merry Christmas!" A crate of oranges, complete with shipping tags, emitted a fragrance that, to Paul at least, was a part of Christmas. Some people were standing near the big iron stove in the middle of the room. There he spotted Kate.

"It's a good thing I have the wagon with me," Paul teased after greeting his sister with an embrace and eyeing the pile of bags and boxes at her side.

"You haven't changed a bit, thank goodness," Kate replied, obviously pleased to see her brother again. "You come alone? I'm anxious to see Nora and the children."

"If we hurry," Paul said, "and get ahead of this storm, you'll see them all for supper. Goodness knows, they've been preparing for your visit. I'm not sure which is most important to them, Christmas or your visit."

Then, as one preoccupied with something other than what he was saying, Paul told Kate, "You stay here by the stove and soak up all the heat you can while I run and pick up some supplies. Then I'll come back and we'll be on our way."

When he returned to the depot a short time later, the crowd had thinned to only the stationmaster and the train crew, who were warming themselves by the stove and talking with Kate.

"You aren't thinking of going back home in this storm, are you?" queried the stationmaster. "If you're smart, you'll put up in the hotel 'til it blows itself out."

Paul replied that they could not do that. The family would be worrying about them. Besides, it was Christmas Eve and the kids had been looking forward to seeing their aunt for several weeks now. They couldn't be disappointed, especially on Christmas.

The stationmaster and the train crew had elected to

wait out the storm before the return trip to Minneapolis. They thought Paul was "crazy as a loon," to consider leaving. Nevertheless, he and Kate loaded her things into the wagon, placing them under the canvas with the supplies he had bought. Then he helped Kate into the wagon and wrapped her in the wool-lined horsehide robe. She sat on the seat in the front end of the wagon box where the sides would help protect her from the blast of the storm. Shaking snow and ice from his great driving coat, Paul put it on himself. It covered him from his ankles to his temples. Next, he pulled his woolen cap with ear flaps down on his head, leaving only his eyes and nose exposed to the elements. Then, with the stationmaster shaking his head in futile dissuasion, Paul raised his hand in a parting salute and headed the horses toward home.

"How foolish I have been!" thought Paul about an hour later as the horses struggled through the deepening snow. For a while after they had left the depot he had remained confident in his decision. As they had skirted the west end of the lake south of town, the snow had slackened and the storm had seemed to be letting up. But after about an hour on their way, the storm had renewed its anger. The snow, no longer wet and sticky, was now dry and cutting and blew horizontally across their path. Rocks, trees, hummocks, and all other landmarks had become indistinguishable from the rest of the landscape. Everything was now a blurred white. Furthermore, the temperature had plummeted so that Paul's nose, toes, and fingers were beginning to sting with the cold. He was relieved, however, to learn that his sister was still quite snug in the horsehide robe.

In what seemed a very short while, the snow piled ever deeper and was whipped into drifts. The horses were finding it increasingly difficult to pull the wagon. After strug-

gling through an especially large drift, Paul stopped the team for a rest. He climbed down beside them, checked the harnesses, and ran his hand over their legs. Their blankets were wet and caked with frozen snow and sweat. He ran his mittened hands over their faces in a futile attempt to brush the snow, which was coming fast and furious, from their eyelashes and nostrils.

Viewing the wall of wind-driven snow all around him, Paul realized it was presumptuous for him to think he could guide the horses any longer. All familiar landmarks had been obliterated, first by the snow and now also by darkness. He felt they were going generally in the right direction, for the wind was still at their backs. But general direction was not enough. He knew that in this storm they could pass by their own house and never realize it. In this vast landscape, it would be all too easy to miss the small cluster of buildings, haystacks, corn shocks, and woodpiles that made up their homestead. Near panic gripped Paul as he imagined Nora and the children coming upon their frozen bodies in the spring and, maybe, those of Jim and Queen in some receding snowbank.

Then Paul remembered hearing it told that horses, left to themselves, were able to find their way home. So, with a mixed feeling of hope and resignation, he wrapped the end of the reins around the stake at the front of the wagon. Then he thrust his hands, aching from the cold, into his coat and crouched down in the box beside Kate, out of the direct blast of the storm.

Over the shriek of the storm he shouted to his sister, "Now we'll see how good the horses are at getting us home." Kate only nodded. To herself she thought, "Is this to be the end of us?" She recalled stories she had heard of lives lost in blizzards. She thought of Nora and the children,

isolated somewhere out there in that fury, waiting for them to come. She could imagine their disappointment in a failed Christmas reunion; of the terrible anxiety of not knowing whether they were dead or alive.

Kate thought of how the cold must be seeping into her luggage, to the presents she had brought for the family. Probably the oranges, so prettily wrapped as special Christmas goodies, would be frozen. But the books she had chosen so carefully for each of the children would not be affected, unless the wind had forced the powdery snow within their wrappings. She thought of the carpet slippers she had found for Paul and how much she hoped he would be able to enjoy them yet this night. And the shawl she had knit for Nora. "Oh God," she prayed, "may we all be reunited this night."

Because of the storm, darkness came even earlier than usual. Nora lit the oil lamp and set it on the table. Its glow brought a feeling of hope into the deepening gloom. She also put a lighted candle on each of the broad windowsills. "Because it is Christmas Eve," she told the children. But to herself she thought, "To help light the way of the travelers." The mellow glow made the room seem even cozier, as their quiet light was reflected in the china and glass settings waiting on the table for the evening meal.

All preparations for the evening had been completed and rechecked several times. Now, as the hour grew late, even the girls were growing uneasy. Nora, to help herself cope with the anxiety in their hearts suggested ways for the children to keep busy. She thought it would be good for Tom to get the evening milking done and for the girls to refill the woodbox in back of the stove. Tom, of course, would have to go to the barn, but the girls would need only to go into the woodshed attached to the house.

Before Tom left for the barn with the milk pail and lantern, Nora insisted he tie one end of the large coil of rope that was piled in a corner of the woodshed around his waist. As he stepped out into the swirling fury of the storm and headed for the barn, Nora watched the rope uncoil. When it was nearly at its end the rope stopped uncoiling and she made the end secure. She could only hope Tom was in the safety of the barn. Straining to see through the swirling darkness, she glimpsed a dim light moving back and forth. Tom was signaling her with the lantern to acknowledge that he had made it safely. She relaxed knowing that when he had finished milking he could grasp the rope and find his way back to the house.

Now that she had done all that could be done for the time being, Nora allowed herself a bit of reflection on the day. She had been up early with Paul, getting his breakfast and seeing him on his way. They both had commented on the mildness of the morning for that late in December, the day before Christmas. Paul had even laughed about how the elements had played a trick on him. No snow for Christmas, and here he had made a sled for the kids, which was hidden in the barn deep under the hay.

Nora recalled how, when he left, she had watched him for several moments as he and the team had headed north toward the hazy horizon. Upon reaching the Sentinels he had turned and waved to her before descending out of sight into the ravine beyond. Nora had walked back toward the house with a sense of foreboding. She chided herself for this mood, realizing that she always had an uneasy feeling when the two of them were apart out here in this open space.

Now as the snow blasted against the window she recalled that the scene that lay before her this morning had not been very impressive. The house and barn, both built mostly of sod and willow poles and some weathered boards, were drab and colorless on that drab, colorless, overcast morning, as were the stocks of hay, corn fodder, and stove wood piled nearby. Everything looked as if it had recently come from the earth on which it stood and could just as easily become a part of it again.

Things were different, however, inside the little house. The larger of the two rooms, which served as their kitchen, dining room, and gathering space, was really quite cheerful in appearance; especially on this day before Christmas. The walls of their sod house, plastered with clay from the creek bank, had been given a fresh coat of whitewash, creating a sense of light and cleanliness within. Nora was especially pleased with the colorful curtains that she had made for the deeply recessed windows. She had made them from a print material hoarded since the move from Minneapolis.

Preparations for Kate's arrival had been meticulously carried out. After the table had been cleared of the noon meal, the girls had helped their mother spread the white linen tablecloth and set out the "company china." Sara and Jenny had already planned that each of them would sit on either side of Aunt Kate. They had also decided that Pa and Ma and Aunt Kate would each sit on a real chair. Because she was the youngest, Jenny would sit on the tall wooden box in which the oil lamp had been packed. As planned, Sara and Tom would share the milk bench. These details, like all other aspects of Aunt Kate's visit had been planned ever since Grandma's letter told of her coming for Christmas.

As Tom milked the cow the quiet sound of alternating streams of milk into the pail was all but drowned out by the roar of the storm outside and the creaking and groaning of the barn timbers. Finishing the milking, Tom gave some of the warm milk to Mordecai the cat and some he poured into a bucket for the calf. Having done these things he took the lantern from its hook and went about inside the barn checking on the other creatures that were in his care on this stormy night. He thought how cozy it really was in that makeshift barn, even though the storm seemed intent on tearing it apart.

"Now," thought Tom, "if only Jim and Queen were in their stalls and Pa and Aunt Kate were safe in the house with the rest of us."

It seemed an eternity since Paul had given up the reins allowing the horses to find their way home by whatever extra senses they might have. He regretted bitterly his decision at the depot to "make for home." He even regretted leaving home that morning, but how was he to have known there would be such a turn in the weather? He thought of his family, alone on that storm-swept prairie, and wondered

how they were faring. Was there enough stove wood stacked in the lean-to shed to see them through? What about the cow, would Tom get her into the barn all right?

The wagon lurched and bumped along over a terrain that could not be seen. The horses stumbled through the ever-changing drifts, sometimes nearly falling as they groped their way. Both passengers in the wagon, keeping their thoughts to themselves, were beginning to feel the effects of the intense cold. Paul thought once that maybe they should get out and follow along behind the wagon to get their blood circulating, but then decided he would rest a while longer; he was beginning to feel drowsy.

Suddenly there was a jolt to the wagon so severe that the two of them huddled on the bottom of the wagon box were thrown against the opposite side. It seemed for a moment that the wagon would overturn, and in the fury of the wind and snow a large piece of tree bark fell upon them. The horses stopped and Paul saw that they had grazed the side of a large tree. He climbed down out of the wagon to see if he could assess the damage. As near as he could tell in the darkness and the storm the only hurt was to the tree, a large cottonwood.

When Paul realized it was a large cottonwood with which they had collided, hope suddenly sprang up within him. He made his way around to the other side of the wagon, reaching out into the storm for what he hoped he would find. After only a few steps through the swirling wind and snow his cold hands made contact with another tree—another large cottonwood.

"Kate," Paul shouted into the storm, "these are the Sentinels! We're almost home! The horses have brought us almost home!"

Paul had to repeat for his sister what he had shouted into the wind. Some of what he had said she didn't understand: "The Sentinels?" But she did understand that those blessed dumb beasts had brought them almost home.

Paul encouraged the horses on into the maelstrom of wind, snow, and darkness. He fully realized that they could still miss the small cluster of objects that represented their home in that stormy expanse of prairie. It was all Paul could do not to take the reins and try to guide the horses to where

he could not see. He must have faith, he thought, that since they had brought them this far they would complete the job and bring them safely to their door.

But Paul was wrong. After what seemed an eternity the two nearly exhausted horses stopped in their tracks. Try as he might he could not get them to move on. Finally in desperation Paul leaped from the wagon and went around to see if he could lead them, to encourage them to move forward. But as he took hold of the two horses' bridles and attempted to pull on them he suddenly became aware of an obstruction in front of them. He reached out and touched it. It was the barn door. The horses had not taken them to the house door but to their own door.

No reunion was ever happier than the one that took place that night. That little sod home, tense with hours of fear and concern, suddenly exploded into a scene of action and emotion as Paul and Kate, caked with snow and ice, stumbled through the woodshed into the kitchen. Eager hands helped them out of their frozen wraps, amidst much talking, laughing, and crying as pent-up emotions were released. Nora brought warm water in which to soak their frostbitten fingers and toes.

No one seemed to mind the mess of melting snow and dripping wraps that were strewn about what had previously been a neat, orderly room. Snow was brushed from Kate's luggage and the boxes and packages taken from the wagon. Then Nora took up a slightly overcooked supper while the children put the wrapped gifts Kate had brought with the others waiting under the window. A Christmas tree would have sat there if they had been able to secure one in this treeless land.

Taking their places around the table that night, Nora breathed a silent prayer and thanked God that all the places were filled. Then all heads bowed as Paul gave his usual table prayer of thanksgiving and petition for guidance and protection in this new land. To each bowed head around that table the words had special meaning.

When they raised their heads, little Jenny piped up, "I think we should all go out to the barn and thank Jim and Queen for the wonderful Christmas gift they brought us tonight."

The Original Christmas Store

SALLY GRAUER

Christmas as the celebration of the birth of Christ brings the joyous strains of favorite carols and special candlelit worship services. It also brings beautifully decorated trees, brightly colored lights, and presents for all.

All the commercial trappings of Christmas seem to be an American phenomenon, setting us apart from the European traditions and those of the rest of the world. A typical American Christmas includes the hustle and bustle of shopping to find a special gift for everyone on the list. It means baking dozens of gaily decorated cookies for family and friends. It involves decorating the house with Christmas greenery and trimming the family tree together. It is the peculiar blending of traditions from one's own childhood with those of family and friends.

We all carry into adulthood treasured symbols of Christmases past. Whether it's a special ornament handed down from our grandparents or a specific kind of tree we prefer, these Christmas symbols are important to us. And so are presents. From the shopping and wrapping and hiding of presents to the squeals of delighted children and the satisfied smiles of adults, we find a particular

joy in the commercial side of Christmas.

We've come a long way from the pilgrims who once banned the celebration of Christmas. Now, year-round Christmas stores are a growing phenomenon. Year-round Christmas stores are springing up all over the country. They can be found in Washington, D.C., Dallas, Texas, Santa Fe, New Mexico.

But the original Christmas store that began business more than 30 years ago is Bronner's Family CHRISTmas Wonderland in Frankenmuth, Michigan. Their doors are open 361 days a year. No business is done on New Year's Day, Easter, Thanksgiving, and Christmas Day, and the store closes from noon until 3:00 on Good Friday.

Have you ever wondered what a modern-day Santa Claus might look like? Probably he would wear a red blazer with a sprig of holly on the lapel, and green trousers. His tie would be black with edelweiss blossoms embroidered on it. Add gold rimmed glasses and white sideburns, a ready smile and the ability to offer greetings to folks in 40 languages, and you have . . . Santa Claus? Could be. Actually, you have described Wally Bronner, the man behind

Bronner's Family CHRISTmas Wonderland.

The store is located on the outskirts of Frankenmuth, a tiny Michigan community that looks like a transplanted bit of Bavaria. The building is done in authentic Bavarian-Alpine architectural style, in keeping with the community. Its address is 25 Christmas Lane.

The landscape surrounding the store includes spruce and balsam trees, Michigan holly, and bright flowers. Delicate edelweiss blooms in season. As you approach the store, you pass a giant snowman and a huge Santa Claus figure. Near the entrance a life-size nativity scene is set in a beautiful natural background of rocks and foliage.

Bronner's is famous for its welcome sign. Visitors are greeted in more than 50 languages, including Swahili. And always more languages are being added. At the exit, another multilingual sign wishes visitors, "See You Again" and "God Bless You."

Still another sign near the entrance sums up Wally Bronner's personal and business philosophy:

ENJOY CHRISTmas!
It's His birthday!
ENJOY LIFE!
It's His way!

Overlooking the large parking lot is a giant clock with months of the year instead of hours. It lets visitors know whether it's half past April or nearly December.

But once you enter the red door of Bronner's, it doesn't matter whether it's July and 90 degrees or a snowy day in November. Inside is the magic world of Christmas.

The showroom pulsates with a riot of colors, sounds, and constant motion against a background of continuous Christmas carols. Twinkling lights dance about the room, refracted by big mirrored balls hanging from the ceiling. Animated displays move in timed motion. Santas, elves, dancing bears, and many other scenes vie for attention.

The enormous showroom covering 40,000 square feet is laid out like a European street fair. Every inch of space is filled with merchandise from floor to high peaked ceiling.

Following Bavarian tradition, the saleswomen dress in German dirndls —a white blouse with a green jumper and a bright red apron. The salesmen wear white shirts, dark green slacks, and red vests. All are pleasant and ready to help in any way. But they are careful always to use the "soft sell" approach. Absolutely no pressure is put on the customer to make purchases.

The average "walk through" of the Christmas fantasyland takes about two hours. That really just covers the basics. There's so much to see that it's impossible to take it all in at one time. Many people come back again and again, even making a visit to Bronner's an annual event in order to add to their Christmas treasures.

The showroom reflects the season's worldwide appeal. Many countries are represented by special items for sale. There's even an American Corner especially designed for the foreign visitor. Here one can find Christmas ornaments in red, white, and blue.

Bronner's boasts of a collection of "Merry Christmas" ornaments with the familiar greeting available in 61 languages. Research continues so that more may be added.

A real "bread and butter" item at the Christmas store is the vast selection of ornaments. Some 3000 styles

are available. Personalized ornaments are always in demand. More than 50,000 ornaments are hand-lettered by Bronner's staff each year. In addition to 150 stock name ornaments, any name or message can be obtained by special order.

Wally began his own design studio for making ornaments after a trip to Europe 18 years ago. Searching for religious ornaments, he found only a few forms of churches and angels. So he decided to develop his own. One technique Wally uses is wire over glass with a nativity scene inside.

Doris Reda has been on Bronner's staff for more than 20 years. She designs many of the ornaments for production in Europe. "We come out with numerous new ornaments each year," she said. "Our goal is to keep Christ foremost in Christmas." Many of the religious ornaments are screen printed to keep them as affordable as possible.

Almost half of the showroom is devoted to a small forest of artificial Christmas trees, tastefully decorated with twinkling lights and decorations. Each tree presents a specific theme. "We can coordinate ornaments for the tree complete with treetop decoration," Doris Reda explained. "If someone wants a decorator tree, we can supply the trimmings."

Each tree is a work of art. The Crystal and Lace Tree is all done with white roses, lace bows, and white lights. The Yum Yum Tree is decorated with ornaments that look exactly like chocolate. And Baby's First Christmas is a treasure done in pink and blue.

There are also trees representing a number of foreign countries. The Scandinavian Tree is decorated with candles, red apples, and straw ornaments, while the Bavarian Tree displays elegant German glass ornaments.

As is true with all the staff at Bronner's, Doris takes great pride in her work. "As I buy ornaments, I try to keep themes in mind. It's a constant challenge," she went on. "We listen to employees and also to the public for ideas. It's a never ending joy."

Wally shows a lot of faith in his staff. Many of their suggestions were incorporated into the new building. The job training period is informal and geared to individual need. "We appreciate the differences in people," Wally commented. Many of the staff are capable of working everywhere in the store. And each department stocks its own shelves.

Still another special part of Bronner's is the Program Center. It seats 200 people and is used for meetings and presentations. It also houses Bronner's Hummel collection. More than 300 little figurines are displayed in a portrayal of the four seasons. A wonderful old parlor pump organ is kept there as well, and every year, a few days before Christmas, the Bronners have a "Sing-along Christmas Caroling." Wally leads the singing and his wife, Irene, plays the organ.

Bronner's is very much a family business. Wally is General Manager and his wife, Irene, is Co-manager. Their children began careers at Bronner's by assembling boxes and packing merchandise. Now son Wayne and daughter Carla work as Assistant General Managers. Lorene, Wayne's wife, is also on the management team.

The store itself grew from rather humble beginnings. Wally first began making Christmas decorations in his father's basement in 1945. He was doing well as a sign painter and

window trimmer following college. By 1951, Wally had added Christmas decorations for cities to his list of accomplishments. In that same year he married his future co-manager, Irene Pretzer. They met at a church youth group.

Creating Christmas decorations for small cities proved a good business. So good in fact that Wally hired a friend who needed a job and the two of them began visiting cities in Michigan, Ohio, Indiana, and Ontario, trying to sell their services. They found a large, hungry market.

In 1952, the Bronners rented a vacant one-room schoolhouse, which became the first permanent year-round display of Christmas decorations.

In the beginning, only the large commercial decorations were sold. But as representatives from cities came to Bronner's, they requested decorations for their own businesses as well. So, a line of decorations for shopping malls and business interiors was added.

Next came a complete line of religious decorations. Then city committees were able to purchase seasonal displays for all commercial areas as well as filling the needs of their own churches.

It was only natural that requests for individual home decorations should follow. Thus, a complete line of decorations for the home was added as well as unique gift items for all seasons, reasons, and budgets.

Bronner's Family CHRISTmas Wonderland continued to grow and prosper. During the years from 1952 to 1977, it outgrew four locations. More and more customers made their way to Bronner's for their Christmas decorating needs.

Wally's strong religious faith is an integral part of the business. He quotes the Bible as easily as business statistics. A packet containing a brochure about Bronner's, one about personalized ornaments, and a religious tract goes out with every purchase and piece of mail.

The advertising for Bronner's Christmas store is an interesting combination. About 70 percent of the paid advertising is through giant billboards in Michigan, Ohio, Indiana, Wisconsin, and Florida. The other 30 percent is through newspaper and travel publications and television spots. "Ninety percent of the store's publicity comes from word of mouth," Wally explained. "People go out and tell their friends and family."

That certainly must be true. The governor of Michigan declared Bronner's an Embassy of Michigan Tourism, a honor Wally is very proud to display.

Christmas year around? It is at Bronner's. And the following facts and figures indicate that many people enjoy what Bronner's offers.

- More than two million people visit Bronner's each year.

- Visitors come from the United States, Canada, and some 30 foreign countries.

- Bronner's is the country's leading supplier of commercial Christmas decorations, stocking over 30,000 individual items.

- Bronner's has the largest collection of nativity scenes in the country, more than 500 in all.

So, does all this make Christmas commercial? It certainly adds that dimension to our Christmas celebrations. And, perhaps, that just makes the joyous season of Christmas even more special.

Our Christmas

Christmas Eve _____

_____

_____

_____

Christmas Day _____

_____

_____

_____

Christmas Worship _____

_____

_____

Christmas Guests   Christmas Gifts

_____   _____

_____   _____

_____   Christmas   _____

_____   Photo   _____

_____   _____

_____   _____

_____   _____

_____   _____

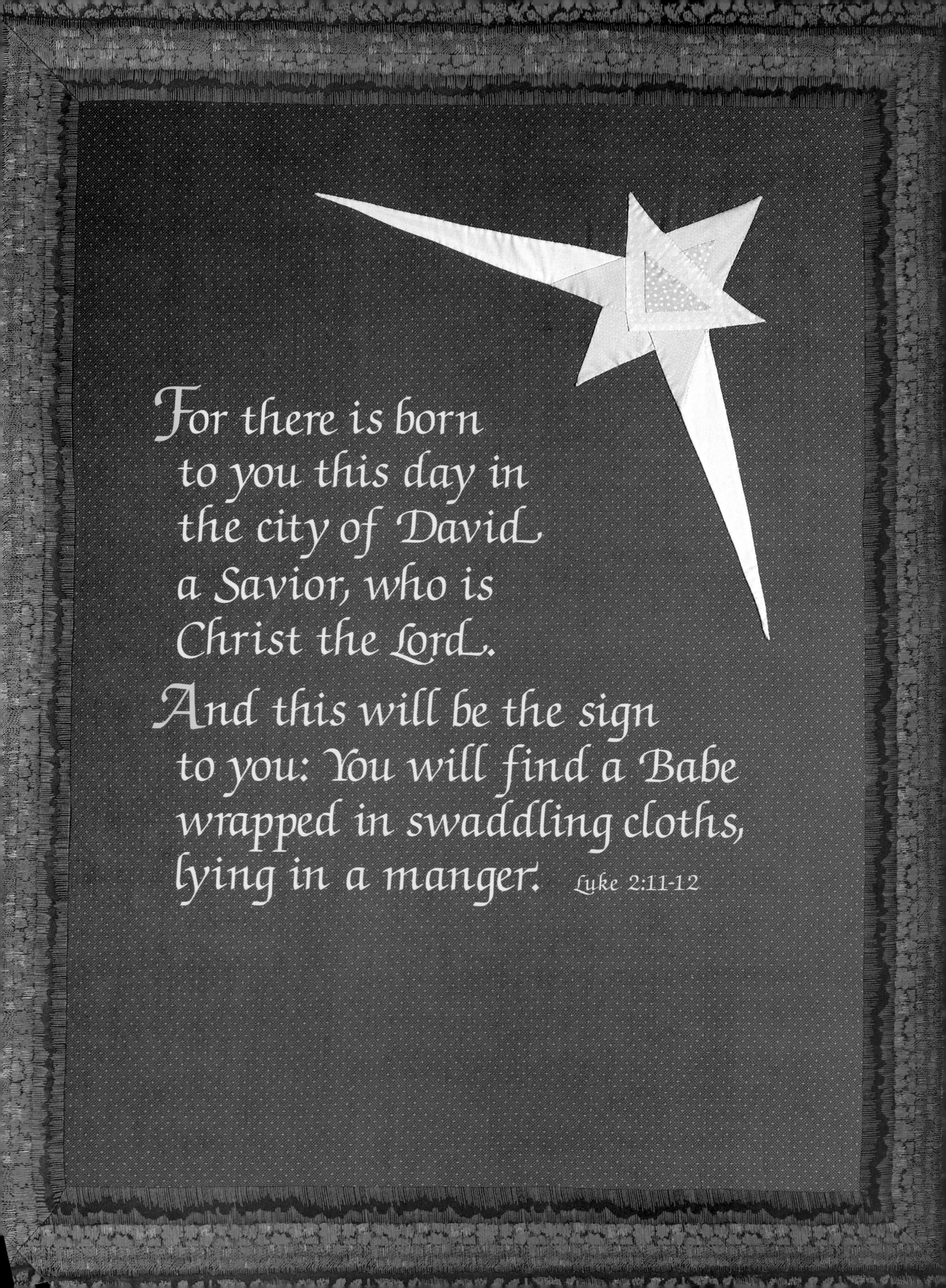

For there is born
to you this day in
the city of David
a Savior, who is
Christ the Lord.
And this will be the sign
to you: You will find a Babe
wrapped in swaddling cloths,
lying in a manger. Luke 2:11-12